Praise

'*Always Free* is amazing. It somehow manages to drip feed very complex information in a very simple way. The book helps you unpick how to actually achieve your financial goals, step by step. Jason is quite magical in that he has been able to help me understand complex topics like investing, by breaking them down into small elements that I can apply quickly and easily. I've worked out that I'm about seventy grand better off than I would have been all in the space of around six or seven months since learning and applying this stuff.'
   — **Dan Moscrop**, Branding Specialist,
   CEO THEM

'I've spent my career building software systems that scale businesses. Jason Graystone's work focuses on building financial systems that scale lives. His guidance in this book took me from surviving to thriving; debt-free, with diversified revenue streams, a clear path to long-term wealth and, most importantly, a renewed sense of direction. While his expertise lies in delivering practical, actionable and proven frameworks for wealth-building, his true genius is in revealing how financial freedom and purpose amplify one another to create a life that truly inspires.'
   — **Paul McGillivray**, Cofounder of Remote. online, Author of *Scope to Scale*

'Jason is my go-to man when it comes to wealth building. I always learnt well because I work hard, but often I didn't use my money wisely or think about the future enough, so my hard work paid off, long-term. Thanks to *Always Free*, I have many wealth building habits that are helping me create a future of freedom and inspiration.'
 — **Ben Coomber**, CEO Awesome Supplements

'Learning from Jason has been nothing short of life changing. The comprehensive nature of the book touches on every aspect of financial independence, from paying off debt and mastering the fundamentals of investing, to building wealth sustainably, launching a personal brand and even starting your own business. The strategies I've learned have not only transformed my finances but positively impacted every area of my life. One of the most impressive aspects of the book is the depth and detail it goes into. Jason's relaxed yet highly accountable teaching style keeps you focused on the ultimate goal: achieving true freedom. His guidance has allowed me to pay off my debts, invest wisely using proven qualitative and quantitative analysis and establish a healthy, positive relationship with money. Beyond that, the book is about building wealth the right way, not just for me but for my family. I now have the tools and knowledge to pass on to my children, accelerating their financial journeys in ways I never thought possible.'
 — **Gregg MacDonald**, Police Officer

'After going bankrupt, discovering *Always Free* was nothing short of life changing. In the first year of applying the Always Free philosophies, I managed to 10x my wealth; a result I never thought possible. However, what I've gained extends far beyond financial success. The teachings in this book have completely transformed my mindset and approach to life. I'm now stronger, fitter, wiser, and I've rebuilt my life with a sense of purpose and clarity that was once unimaginable. Most importantly, for the first time, I know exactly when I will be free, and that certainty has fuelled my drive to achieve more than I ever thought possible. *Always Free* didn't just help me recover; it gave me the tools to build a life that inspires me every day. I'm living proof of the power of Always Free. Thank you for everything.'

— **Daniel Sirdar**, Data Manager

'I found *Always Free* so inspiring, so helpful and so life changing. The content is like doing a degree – it has allowed me to really home in on what I want to do with the rest of my life and how I can create my own financial freedom. Within six months of applying what I learned, my life is changing. Thank you, Jason.'

— **Jenny McDonald**, The Food Freedom Fairy

'*Always Free* made me think about my long-term goals, what I want to do, where I want to be and what I want to create. In a short space of time, I've managed to manufacture a makeup line and got my

coaching program up running; there's no way in a million years I would have done that without Jason's teachings in *Always Free*. It's changed me massively as a person in business and personally, as well.'
　— **Essjay Hartshorn**, Beauty Business Coach

'The basic structure of principles in *Always Free* has truly, truly changed my life. Jason has had such a positive impact on my life – I'm financially free and I have peace of mind. Definitely. It was a serious deal. I learned how to be an adult with my money thanks to Jason.'
　— **Chloe Bourjalliat**, Certified Fitness and
　　Performance Coach

ALWAYS FREE

How to become financially free to live an inspired life

JASON GRAYSTONE

R^ethink

First published in Great Britain in 2025 by Rethink Press (www.rethinkpress.com)

© Copyright Jason Graystone

All rights reserved. No part of this publication may be reproduced, stored in or introduced into a retrieval system, or transmitted, in any form, or by any means (electronic, mechanical, photocopying, recording or otherwise) without the prior written permission of the publisher.

The right of Jason Graystone to be identified as the author of this work has been asserted by him in accordance with the Copyright, Designs and Patents Act 1988.

This book is sold subject to the condition that it shall not, by way of trade or otherwise, be lent, resold, hired out, or otherwise circulated without the publisher's prior consent in any form of binding or cover other than that in which it is published and without a similar condition including this condition being imposed on the subsequent purchaser.

Disclaimer

The views expressed in this book do not constitute financial advice. The investment ideas discussed should never be used without first assessing your own financial situation and consulting a qualified financial adviser. Neither the author nor the publisher can be held responsible for any losses that may result from investments made after reading this book.

Thank you to my son Harrison. Nobody trains anyone how to be a parent, but as soon as you were born, I became focused, driven, inspired and motivated to provide you with the best opportunities in life. Without you, I would not have had the drastic mind shift that changed my entire path in life. My second son Ethan strengthened my focus and you both are my why for everything I do.

I am grateful also to my wonderful wife Sarah, without whose support and trust in me going against the norm, I would have questioned my own actions at times. By allowing me to chase my dreams, you have enabled us to create one of the most mutually respectful and successful relationships I have known. Thank you.

Finally, thank you to everyone who has the courage to choose for themselves. Everyone who dares to question the status quo. Everyone who believes that they deserve to make the most of their life on this rock and everyone who has the courage to live their life on their terms. Everyone who wants to become a better human being.

Contents

Foreword	1
Introduction	5
My story	6
Questioning the status quo	8
In a nutshell	13
PART 1 Setting the Record Straight	**15**
1 Creating Your Mental Freedom	**19**
Be selfish first	20
Your beliefs hold you back	22
Altruism vs narcissism	24
Beware	29
It's time for take off	33
2 Get Your Mind Right	**35**
The writing's on the wall	36
Watch your language	39

The flow of money	40
Identifying your vision	42
Process over outcome	45

PART 2 Home Truths — 47

3 Question Everything — 49
Don't respect your elders	51
Challenge the status quo	51
Everyone has an agenda	54

4 Money Myths — 57
Money is time	59
Time is your most valuable asset	61
Self-worth	64

5 Net Worth Is Not Wealth — 67
What are your goals?	68
Millionaires can still have money worries	71
The millionaire and the paperboy	73

6 Look Within — 79
People do not want you to succeed	81
My lightbulb moments	83
It's all about you	87

PART 3 A Glimpse of Reality   91

7 Exploring Your Self-Worth   93

   Know your purpose and structure your life around it   95

   Your values dictate your financial destiny   98

8 Taking Control Of Your Life   103

   Quality questions   105

   You will never please everyone   109

   Money is nothing but a tool of opportunity   111

9 Your Route To Financial Freedom   117

   Planning for financial freedom   118

   A note about debt   125

10 Mobility Freedom – Designing Your Inspired Life   133

   Delegation   135

   Your focus for guaranteed financial freedom   137

   Time to set a benchmark   141

   The path to financial freedom   151

PART 4 The Tiers of Financial Freedom WEALTH Method©   153

11 What And Why?   155
    The importance of specific goals   156
    Finding your why   158

12 Expenses And Expectations   163
    Stop the bleeding   164
    Prioritising your savings   170
    Creating your wealth liquidity system   179
    Reducing debt   190

13 Asset Accumulation   195
    Part I – Cash buffer comforts   196
    Part II – Investing to grow your wealth   205
    Part III – Earning your right to risk   214
    Part IV – Intelligent investing   230

14 Leveraged Income   249
    Income growth   251
    Types of income   253
    Ways to improve your income   255

15 Trading   259
    Part I – Why trading?   262
    Part II – Risk appetite   274

16	**Hedging**	**287**
	Investing to speculation ratio	289
	Capital partitioning	294
	Accelerating financial freedom	296

PART 5   Becoming Always Free — 299

17	**Scaling Your Lifestyle**	**301**
	The FREEDOM lifestyle scale formula	302
18	**The Time Is Now**	**307**
	Dissolving your excuses	309
	Hard work is a myth	314
	Take action	315

Conclusion: The Key Is Happiness	**319**
The three freedoms	321
The Author	**325**

Foreword

Everyone has a unique hierarchy of values or set of priorities that shape their perceptions, decisions and actions. In my experience, one of the deepest yearnings across this hierarchy in most individuals is the desire for freedom – particularly financial freedom. This craving is not just about accruing wealth, but about securing the liberty to pursue one's most inspiring objectives and live in alignment with one's highest values without financial constraint.

True freedom, however, is often misconceived. It is not merely the absence of financial limitations or obligations, but rather the freedom and presence of choices – the ability to engage in activities that are inspiring and meaningful and ones aligned with one's most intrinsic values. People want to feel free to express themselves, to expand their horizons, and to contribute meaningfully without being hindered by economic limitations.

Always Free delves into this nuanced understanding of freedom. It unravels the psychological and practical dimensions of financial empowerment and how these can be harnessed to achieve not just monetary wealth, but a deeply fulfilling life of freedom. Through its pages, this book debunks immediately gratifying financial speculations, fantasies and schemes, and instead offers profound insights into aligning your financial strategies with your highest values, thus enhancing your potential for both wealth creation and inner satisfaction.

Moreover, the strategies and philosophies espoused in *Always Free* guide you to a deeper comprehension of what it means to be truly free. The book teaches you how to master your finances rather than be enslaved by them. It encourages you to look beyond the superficial allure of money and to see wealth as a tool for crafting a life rich with purpose and meaning.

As you traverse through this enlightening narrative, you will discover that financial freedom is not an end in itself but a means to live your most inspired life. It is about creating a life where your financial resources serve not as chains that bind you, but as wings that help you soar towards your highest aspirations.

I have been in Jason's company many times over the years and I commend him for his dedication to empowering others through this valuable work. *Always Free* is more than a written guide; it is a catalyst for transformation for anyone who dares to redefine the boundaries of their financial and individual human potential. May this book inspire you to take bold steps towards a life of true freedom, where your financial achievements and individual fulfilment are in perfect harmony.

Credit to Jason Graystone.

Dr John Demartini, International best-selling author of *The Values Factor*[1]

---

1 Dr JF Demartini, *The Values Factor: The secret to creating an inspired and fulfilling life* (Penguin, 2013)

Introduction

Think back to when you were seven years old. It's Saturday morning. What were you doing? Would you be playing ball games? Would you be with your friends? Would you rush off to get a comic, some sweets, maybe an ice cream?

That, in its purest form, was freedom: mental freedom to be yourself, mobility freedom to move and play and no financial burden weighing you down.

Then we saw the adults and thought, 'Oh my, when I get to be an adult, I will be in control. I cannot wait! Nobody can tell me when to go to bed or tell me what to do or anything. I will be free.'

The thing is, we had *all* the freedom we could dream of; we just didn't see it at the time.

It's hard to appreciate that without hindsight at seven years old, of course, but when we became adults, suddenly we were being more controlled than ever. We'd lost the sense of freedom.

So many adults have ended up being less free, more controlled and as far as possible from who we really were and are. We almost completely lose the one thing we are born with, our freedom.

Everyone wants the freedom we all once had, yet most people never achieve it. Why is that?

This book is going to answer that question. I am going to show you how to get your freedom back. This book is your guide to reclaiming them, and redefining what it truly means to be free again.

Always Free.

My story

Firstly, to get off on the right foot, I want to say that I am not an inventor, an academic, a university graduate or a scholar. I'm just a regular guy with an inquisitive mind who figured out some stuff that has allowed me to live a remarkable life completely on my terms.

I was born on 20 October 1981. My dad had already left. My mum was broke. We lived on a council estate until I was eighteen years old and I had no guidance, no accountability and no close role models.

When I was five years old, I was babysat by one of south London's most notorious gangster families while my mum tried to make ends meet working various part-time jobs. The year I hit thirteen, my biological father was stabbed, beaten, shot in the face with a sawn-off shotgun and hospitalised before being housed in a secret location after a life of gangster crime.

My English teacher made a mockery of me in front of the entire class when he insisted I stand up as he said that I would 'fail at life' if I didn't grasp the script for William Shakespeare's comedic play *Much Ado About Nothing*. While we're on the topic of school, my economics teacher said I was wasting my talent by being easily distracted and playing the class clown, and during the final year of school I was bullied, which resulted in me failing all of my exams except art.

I was a pretty disengaged student at school. The only time I managed to resonate with anything or take in information was if someone explained it to me in a way that was so simple, it would stick. I was the kid that didn't get it. I always felt like I was the only one who was not taking in information and much of the time today, I still feel this way. I have never felt clever or intelligent.

Straight out of school, I fell into a job as an electrician, and while training, I repeatedly failed to secure my dream role of becoming a firefighter on the side because I was terrible in interviews. I was a bad communicator.

I was born into a single-parent family moving from one council house to another with no inspirational role models, no guidance and little education. I had no unicorn business idea and no lottery win.

The point is this: I never had anything handed to me on a silver platter, yet I was able to achieve financial independence by the time I was thirty.

Questioning the status quo

Today, I am able to choose how I spend every minute of my time and have enough money coming in each month to fund my happiness without ever having to worry about the cost of comforts and luxuries. I got to this position by doing what I am sharing in *Always Free*.

I wish I'd had this book when I started my journey. It took me far longer to get to this position than it needed to and I spent long periods of time figuring out what didn't work as well as what did.

During my journey, I noticed some important yet predictable patterns with emotions when it came down to how my finances were handled. When I went to work, earnt money and saved as much as I could on a particular month, I would feel good and my mindset was positive. Then there would be months where I would have a big spend and I would feel more stressed as the cash in my bank account dropped. How I handled my income and savings affected my mood and I realised that there was a way to master finances, which in turn helped my mindset.

I made discoveries that allowed me to nail down a solid wealth creation strategy so I could live a life on my terms. A life where I was the pilot. A life where I could spend my time doing what I wanted. A life where I wouldn't ever need to worry about paying the bills. A life where I could provide support for my family. A life that would allow me to identify and create opportunities that would otherwise be passed up and, most importantly, a life that would enable me to spend my time in areas that I find most fulfilling and rewarding while helping others do the same.

Your wealth sweet spot isn't just about money. It's about having the freedom to design a life on your terms so that you can take actions that align with your values. Free to question, free to make your own decisions, free to spend time with who you want, whenever you want, doing what you want. Ultimately, it's about mastering life so that you are rewarded, fulfilled and doing meaningful things.

If you want a great result in something, you must firstly be inspired to learn. Secondly, you must have the ambition and drive to achieve it. *Always Free* will ignite that inspiration, ambition and drive in you as well as giving you strategies for financial freedom.

Always Free combines savings and financial advice, investing, and speculation and trading. Its content is based on what I have learned works and doesn't work through personal experience. By implementing the strategies in this book, you will find that you are actually already capable of incredible things that, if packaged and distributed the right way, can leave a truly meaningful legacy for you and your family.

I have not invented *any* of the strategies. I have simply learned from people, made a lot of mistakes, spent a lot of time and money figuring out what does *not* work, and then used my logical brain to cut through the noise to create an efficient and effective pathway to freedom by forming my own unique principles. I have taken pieces of advice and strategies from hundreds of mentors and copied my way to success. My hope is that you save yourself some valuable time and use this book to do the same.

INTRODUCTION

You are about to learn in hours what took me years.

Some of the concepts may seem like common sense, others may seem contradictory or contrary to what you have believed or heard before. Some things in the book will be profound to you. One thing is for sure, the differences between those who have the life they love and those who don't are outlined in these pages for you to take on board. The pathway to your most inspired life is paved in the chapters and the strategies are there for you to learn, retain and implement.

I won't deny that parts of this book will demand self-review, questioning of your own situation, and at times will feel uncomfortable, but I *promise* you that if you read it to the end and take action on the advice, your life will never quite be the same again.

Developing yourself, expanding your consciousness and pushing life around to suit your destiny is the best thing you can do as a human being. I want you to have your cake and eat it too. In fact, I want you to choose your cake, design it, colour it, flavour it, bake it, decorate it, then systemise the recipe and outsource the baking to create a never-ending stream of delicious cakes that keep showing up so you can eat them with whoever you want, whenever you want, wherever you want, however you want and for as long as you want, until you've had enough.

Most people don't want to be rich; they want to be free.

Free from fear, free from guilt, free from obligation. They want to wake up each day with a clear mind, a meaningful direction and the ability to live on their own terms.

Always Free is a philosophy that defines what that truly means.

It's not just about money or success, it's about achieving three essential freedoms: mental freedom, mobility freedom and financial freedom. When these three align, you unlock your full potential as a human being.

This book is your roadmap to reclaiming control over your mind, your time and your resources so you can live a life of clarity, purpose and complete sovereignty. This isn't a motivational book. It's a measurable, structured journey to the life you were always meant to live.

1. **Mental Freedom**: The ability to think clearly, know who you are and live without the mental baggage of fear, shame, guilt or external expectations. You detach your decisions from societal pressures and idealisms, and operate from self-awareness, integrity and peace of mind. Knowing who you truly are, what you are here for and when enough is enough.

2. **Mobility Freedom**: The freedom to do what you want, where you want, with whom you

want. Your lifestyle and income are designed intentionally, so your work feels like a natural extension of your purpose, not a chore or a chain. Your vocation should inspire you and allow you to serve without being a slave.

3. **Financial Freedom**: The ability to cover your living expenses indefinitely through leveraged or passive income. You convert earned income into assets that produce cash flow, freeing you from the need to 'work for money.'

These freedoms aren't abstract ideals, they are measurable goals. When you begin scoring and improving each, you move closer to the ultimate goal.

To be Always Free is to become the most authentic, inspired and impactful version of yourself. A life free in mind, movement and money. That's the good life.

In a nutshell

When people think about freedom, they usually link it solely to finances. The truth is, there is a little more to it than that.

It starts with a choice. A choice to be:

- Free from social opinions
- Free from judgement

- Free from societal idealisms
- Free to choose
- Free to control
- Free to take action

Always Free is your new mantra.

Imagine earning enough money to cover the lifestyle you dream of while having more time freedom, mobility freedom and mental freedom than ever. Passion, fulfilment, reward.

Sound like a dream outcome?

Guess what, the way you get there is to tackle each of those things. Master them and you get the dream life. That's what it's all about, isn't it?

Happiness. Happiness is simply a choice. I want to help you have that choice.

BOOK TIP

I recommend reading this book while listening to the audiobook at the same time. Not only will you retain the information better, but if you set the audiobook to 1.25x–2.0x speed, you will read faster.

PART 1
SETTING THE RECORD STRAIGHT

When you are true to yourself, you are mentally free, freer than if you won the lottery.

The majority of people do not achieve financial freedom due to lack of strategy and planning, unrealistic expectations, taking poor advice and fantasies about wealth. Often, they look up to others and attempt to live outside their own value system, and then expect to excel in areas of life that really aren't important to them. I see people emulating 'entrepreneurs' or 'traders' or 'celebrities' on social media, fantasising about how the other half live. It's soul destroying. When they do this, they end up feeling negative, depressed, resentful, angry, or all of the above.

Every time you look up to someone, you are blind to the realities of their life and you give your power away. How can you possibly focus on your own financial future by looking at someone else's?

Until now, you may have had a plan for financial freedom that was based on nothing other than a fantasy. From today onwards, let's make your financial freedom a reality.

To do so, first of all, you must read this entire book. Send me an email or a message to let me know you have started and are committed to reading it to the end. Post a picture on social media right now of you with the book and tag me in it, or send me the picture via email or private message if you prefer.

If you wish, I vow to repost your picture to hold you accountable too.

To put my money where my mouth is and show my level of confidence in this book raising your financial intelligence (otherwise known as financial quotient – FQ), I invite you to do a quick test right now, then again at the end to see what a difference *Always Free* has made to your life. Simply go to www.alwaysfree.com/fqtest, answer the questions as well as you can, and then come back here to start shifting your financial destiny.

As we dive into mindset, purpose, income, investing and everything else, I want you to promise me that you will not skip a single word of this book. How you do anything is how you do everything. Give yourself permission to master this now. There is going to be some heavy lifting at the start and this will be more of a workbook for you than a leisurely read, but there is no traffic after the mad mile!

We start with the inner work.

Ready? Let's get stuck in.

1
Creating Your Mental Freedom

You must first understand what freedom is: true freedom and inspiration come from choice.

When we are free to choose, we are free to become better. *Always Free* is not designed to change who you are as a person; instead, it will move you closer to who you already are inside. It will give you the roadmap to your perfect life and the financial strategies that support and underpin that life.

By the time I turned thirty, I was free from a job and free to do whatever I wanted wherever I wanted. I was *Always Free*.

My friends and family were surprised at how much free time I had and would build suspicions about my income. 'Is he dealing drugs?' they would ask. Whenever friends arranged a meal out, gathering or party, the dates and times were set to fit around their schedules because my reply was, 'Just let me know whenever, I'm always free!' This became my motto. I was known for always being free.

I want you to start telling people you are always free. Not so that they can fill your calendar with being a shoulder to cry on and running errands all day; instead, it's an affirmation to live life on your terms. Always free to design a life that allows you to be who you truly want to be. Start now. Make a choice to be always free and we can begin the journey together.

Whenever you don't feel free, you are simply off track from being who you really are.

Be selfish first

As anyone who has ever listened to the safety announcement before flying will know, in the event of an emergency, you must always put your own oxygen mask on before helping others with theirs.

Despite what you may have believed up until this point, it's better to receive than to give. Hear me out.

Living a free and inspired life is about being able to enjoy and experience life to the fullest while also being in the position to help and support your family, friends and community without having to actively exchange valuable time doing uninspiring tasks for money. It's knowing that you can afford to support your kids, treat your friends and family; that you can dedicate time to community initiatives you believe in without feeling as though you have restrictions on your free time.

Whatever freedom looks like for you, the starting point is having a free mind. A mind that is able to make meaningful choices. We are most inspired when we can fill our time with activities and tasks that we choose and love to do. Sacrificing your inspiration to help others is counterproductive and will only get you so far.

I'm not saying helping others is something to be completely ignored, but understand that you can only do so when you are living life to your highest values. When you are free, living authentically and being who you truly want to be, you unlock the most evolved part of the brain that allows us to plan ahead, get creative, deal with judgement, complexity, organisation, and bring more order to our lives, enabling us to make better decisions aligned with our mission and purpose on Earth. You become your own executive! The person in charge of your life.

You will only unlock this part of your brain if you first reach the position of freedom.

You can have all the money in the world, but if other people's judgement determines how you spend it, you will never have a free life that you dream of. This is how lottery winners go broke so quickly. They attempt to buy acceptance from their friends and family to prove they are still 'normal' until all their money is squandered.

You need mental freedom. To help you achieve that, I would like to start by sharing some common beliefs that I have witnessed holding many people back from obtaining their dream life.

Your beliefs hold you back

We all have a belief system that guides our actions, and much of the time, we're unaware of how our beliefs are affecting the way we behave and therefore what we see in our lives.

The belief that giving is better than receiving is one of many you may hold. Statements such as, 'Everything I do is for my family (or kids, or parents)' are highly likely to be stopping you from achieving the life you want. It's ironic, but by believing that everything you are doing is for someone else, you will naturally limit how far you can go before guilt sets in, and you will eventually need to do something highly selfish to get the life you want. Because you have a belief that everything you do is for other people, doing anything for yourself will cause guilt and limit you. The truth is, if you want to do more for your family, your kids, your friends, you have to commit to doing more for yourself.

If you are living the social ideal that you should put others first, stop. It will literally prevent you from being able to excel in your own life, let alone provide for others. It can help you to get over your feelings of guilt when you understand that, primarily, everything you are doing is for yourself. Even when you achieve the life you want, you will at most be doing 50% for others and 50% for yourself. If you provide a house for your family, you will be living there too. If you buy food, you will be eating it too. If you take your partner on holiday, you will be 50% of the travel cost.

I often see people make the mistake of being far too altruistic or giving before they are in the position to do so. They set up charities or non-profit organisations while they can barely afford to pay their own bills.

When you speak with people who are of the opinion that it is better to give than to receive and you dig a little deeper, it usually transpires that they have a rescue complex of some kind. This is normally a result of unresolved guilt in their past which is stopping them from going after what they want because they feel they don't deserve it. Each time they dare to push the threshold, the guilt creeps back in and they give their power to others. Those who experience this also seem to have an extreme view against narcissism.

This topic has become popular during recent years, so I want to address it for myself and for you.

Altruism vs narcissism

Altruism and narcissism are each different sides to the same coin, and you have to embrace both to live an inspired life. Freedom is found in the centre.

Here we will look at these traits and the consequences of each.

Someone who is an extreme narcissist is always out for themselves. They usually want to have money and attention. In other words, fame and fortune. They may have an agenda to benefit themselves at the expense of others.

The problem with the extreme narcissist is they spend so much time focusing on themselves that they forget to serve others. Although they want to chase money and fame, they are usually too neglectful of others to be able to attract real wealth. Extremely narcissistic people have a problem obtaining what they set out for because they always want the spotlight to be on them, and therefore they find it hard to serve the marketplace in any meaningful way. Narcissists normally try to rip people off and do not provide as much value to the world as they are charging for. They end up riddled with guilt and, as a result, unhappy.

Someone who is an extreme altruist always puts others first. They fill the majority of their time with tasks and activities set out by others. They are forever doing favours for people; they are the shoulder to cry on. They actively seek friendship and never want anything in return for their acts of kindness.

The problem with the extreme altruist is they have great ideas and like to serve, but they find it impossible to ask for fair exchange. They struggle immensely in business because they fail to act on their great ideas; they cannot imagine anyone would want to pay for something they create. They avoid asking for the sale and as a result, their business only lasts until the freebies have been soaked up by their social group. Extremely altruistic people usually have a rescue complex of some kind (ie they think they are responsible for helping others) and as a result, they allow themselves to be told what to do by others. They tend to end up resentful and unhappy.

I know people who are extremely narcissistic and people who are extremely altruistic. Both extremes can be destructive or lead to a disempowered life. The key, as always, is balance. However (and this is the part many people struggle with), according to the laws of cause and effect, you have to be more narcissistic initially to ultimately be more selfless and giving. Income is outcome and outcome is income, but there is an order of priority here.

If you give too much too early, you will always be lagging behind in inspiration and fulfilment. If you really want to give as much as you can to the people that you love or a greater cause, you must give yourself permission to go after what you truly want in life and stop listening to societal ideals.

If eradicating the problem of world hunger is not something you really have a burning desire to do, and you are just trying to do it because of someone you are looking up to or social ideals, you will burn out and won't even come close to making a real impact in solving this highly complex issue. If you are not fully committed to achieving peace on Earth, don't try to solve that problem either. You have to align your goals with your passions.

While you're deciding what your passions are, be a bit more narcissistic. If your thoughts are consumed by how you wish there was better education in schools, then go after that. Just know that you will need to put yourself first initially to develop your knowledge and resources to have the greatest positive impact.

Here is what I have observed. The most overly narcissistic people usually turn out to be the most giving philanthropists, and the most altruistic people usually turn out to be selfish. I don't mean selfish in a bad way, but in terms of limiting what they can offer the world, how many people they can reach, what support they can provide for their family and what difference they can make.

Narcissism, then altruism

To live an inspired life, you must embrace both narcissism and altruism, but before you even start to help others, you have to give yourself permission to live by your true values, and that means being slightly more narcissistic.

Understand that if you only ever wanted to travel in a northward direction around the Earth, you would eventually meet a point where you start to travel south. To master financial independence, you must expect to have a mixture of both altruism and narcissism throughout your journey. Throughout this book, I will show you where it's best to focus on your narcissistic tendencies, and where you can let your altruistic traits shine through.

An inspired life requires you to be able to serve others, provide value and ask for fair exchange simultaneously. That doesn't mean you have to have your own business or be an entrepreneur. If you have a job, you must be able to provide value to your company as well as you can and ask for a fair reward at the same time.

Being able to justify your pay rise or bonus by over-delivering in your industry will enable you to scale both your altruism and narcissism. It's the same when it comes to negotiating chores or time on your own with your family so you can all get what you want in life. In other words, this is about working out how much you can give while getting what you need for yourself.

In a relationship dynamic, it means being there for people you love while being able to say no to those who always seem to take and never give anything in return. The balance is in the contribution each partner brings to the relationship.

Pressing the reset button

Why did I say you need to be slightly more narcissistic first? Because most people have the idea that if you do more for yourself than others, you should feel guilty or selfish. You need to reset that way of thinking and understand that if you are to start designing your own life, you have to make choices that are aligned with you first.

Let's look at this through the lens of someone who wants to leave their mark by sharing knowledge and wisdom via quality education. Before they can share with others, they first have to acquire the knowledge and wisdom themselves. In the same way, a person who wants to teach others how to become financially free cannot possibly do so without first achieving the result themselves.

They are narcissistic to then be altruistic. It's like me becoming *Always Free* before writing this book for you to read.

The lesson here is that you need to put yourself first while you embark on your development in the particular area or field you love and choose.

Beware

The more you push towards your goals, the more you will find that there are people trying to pull you back to the status quo. Mastering the balance between give and take is going to require you to be aware of when to push or pull. It's like a see-saw or a tug-o-war.

You are going to have to accept that to get to where you want to be, you may have to let a few people go and be your own best friend for a while. Remove yourself from the naysayers, doubters and the ones that always want a shoulder to cry on but never offer a shoulder of their own. Beware of the ones who thrive on doom and gloom. Beware of those who tell you that you are fine the way you are and you should be happy with life. These are the people who will say things like, 'There is more to life than money' or 'You are so busy chasing your dream that you are forgetting what life is about'.

Really?

These statements normally come from people who think they aren't selfish when in fact, they are being extremely selfish. They just don't see it. They have short time and space horizons. The impact and difference you make in the world, the level of complexity and chaos you can bring order to, the amount of income you generate, the influence you can have, the legacy you leave are all correlated to your time and space horizons.

For example, factory workers are usually able to think about their responsibilities day-to-day. They know what the job at hand is, are only responsible for themselves and are paid a relatively low wage accordingly. A factory manager might be able to think week-to-week to manage a team, deal with conflict and command leadership, and as a result is paid more than the shop-floor workers. A factory CEO will be thinking month-to-month about the profit and loss, the future of the business, recruitment, partnerships, a high level of chaos and complexity, and as a result will be paid more than the manager. A visionary will be thinking year-to-year or decade-to-decade.

You get the point. The further you can visualise the future, the more order you bring to your life, the more inspired you become and the more money you attract.

As I stated earlier, true wealth is being able to support and help your friends, family and community while experiencing life to the fullest. The wealthier you become, the more people you can support, and the more caring, loving and understanding you will be.

What would your life look like now if you didn't need money? I'm not just talking about your job, but how would you speak to people? What would you put up with and not put up with? How would you talk to your customers? What products or services would you create? Who could you support?

The time will come when you will be living your best life. When you get there, you will be able to support others to a much higher degree.

If your parents or loved ones become ill and need care, you can be the one who is there to help. If your family members need financial support, you can supply it. If you decide to raise children, you will be in the best position to support them mentally and financially. If you wish to raise money for a charity or make a difference in the world, you can. You can make a greater difference by helping more people and for a longer time.

The people who said you were being selfish will then be the ones who have little to offer. While being busy in the mindset of 'There is more to life', *they* have unknowingly become more and more selfish, and limited themselves as a result.

You have a choice

Without doubt, it can be difficult to say no, to swim against the tide, to shut out friends and family who have a fixed mindset for the short term, but it is absolutely necessary if it means you will reach your goal quickly, which in turn allows you to live your dream life of inspiration for the time you are here on this Earth. The early stages of the journey are usually the hardest. You are faced with doubt, guilt, dread, gossip, jealousy and even spite; but honestly, there is no time to worry about that.

You are here on this Earth once. Don't you think you deserve to choose how you spend your time? It has taken millions of years to get to a point which gave you 400 trillion-to-one odds of being alive as a human.[2] Isn't it silly to spend a minute worrying about what other people think of you or letting them tell you what to do?

It is! How many summers or Christmas holidays do you have left? You don't have time to worry. Let's get to work.

It's time for take off

When NASA first sent astronauts to the moon, the landing was a milestone for humankind. However, the actual landing wasn't the hardest part. To make history, the hardest thing to do was to accelerate past the pull of gravity.

Although the gravitational force kept the astronauts' world safe and in order, they knew that to achieve their mission, they had to surpass this barrier of comfort and that once they did, the rest would be free sailing. Finding the energy required to go against everything that was common and face the unknown was the obstacle the crew had to break through.

Your most inspired life is waiting beyond the constraints of your own atmosphere. Often when you examine it, you will realise it's an atmosphere created

---

2   Dr A Binazir, 'Are you a miracle? On the probability of your being born' (Huffpost, 16 August 2011), www.huffpost.com/entry/probability-being-born_b_877853, accessed 17 October 2024

by other people's opinions and fears of rejection and failure. The way to break through this is to give yourself permission now. Be who you want to be. Be selfish in your actions now and you will be selfless in your cause later on.

TOP TIP

To be good at anything requires discipline, focus, effort and, sometimes, a little sacrifice. To get to where you want to be, you will first need to get good at saying no to anything that doesn't align with your bigger mission. Be selfish. If you don't fill your time with tasks and actions that inspire you, it will get filled with tasks and actions that don't. Other people will fill your time with their agenda.

2
Get Your Mind Right

If you don't have control of your mind, you will never be free.

I have already stressed the importance of your mindset, but before we go any further, I would like to explain why it's so important to have the right mindset as you start your journey to financial freedom, and also what mindset you need to cultivate. Make no mistake, choosing to pursue financial freedom is a big decision that requires a great deal of courage. Financial freedom isn't something most people have, and that means to achieve it, you will need to do what most people don't. You have to go against the status quo, which means you also have to get used to people doubting you and telling you that you're wrong.

'If you ever receive a million pounds, you'd better work out how to be a millionaire so you get to keep the money' sums up the importance of mindset. You need to develop the right mindset to manage the emotions that come from accepting wealth and freedom. This comes back to the concept that you have to be comfortable doing what most people will tell you is the wrong thing to do.

The writing's on the wall

According to the Department for Work and Pensions, the average retirement age in the UK is sixty-seven at the time of writing[3] and slowly pushing upwards. According to the Office for National Statistics, the average life expectancy in the UK is 78.6 for men and 82.6 for women.[4]

The average UK pension pot balance (if people even have a pension) at the age of retirement is £37,000.[5] If we were to view retirement as being 12.5 years, this pension

---

3   Department for Work and Pensions, State Pension age Review 2023 (Gov.UK), www.gov.uk/government/publications/state-pension-age-review-2023-government-report/state-pension-age-review-2023, accessed 17 October 2024
4   Office for National Statistics, National life tables – life expectancy in the UK: 2020–2022, www.ons.gov.uk/peoplepopulationandcommunity/birthsdeathsandmarriages/lifeexpectancies/bulletins/nationallifetablesunitedkingdom/2020to2022, accessed 17 October 2024
5   A Williams, 'What does a pension pot worth £37,000, £150,000 and £500,000 give you?', *The Times* (25 March 2025), www.thetimes.com/money-mentor/pensions-retirement/private-pension/pension-pot-amount-average-uk-how-much, accessed 15 April 2025

pot would mean that in the 'golden years' when people should be enjoying the fruits of their labour, the majority of them actually have to live on around £1,160 per month. Do you think that is possible? When you sit down and let that sink in, it's extremely eye opening and alarming. What's more alarming is how small a number of people actually bother to do the maths.

Then there's the impact of inflation. Every twenty-five years, the cost of living doubles (depending on your country's inflation rate).[6] This is not to mention that once you retire with a pension, you will have more free time, which means you will have more time to spend.

After working for forty-five years, some people end up with enough money to cover just one to two years' worth of expenses before they become a burden. They have to hope they don't live beyond seventy-nine because their pension pot will then run out of money, or hope they have other family members who can support them for the rest of their days.

That's no way to live, is it? It's disempowering. No one wants to be a burden to anyone no matter how close you are with friends or family.

It fascinates me how little effort people invest into their future, often thinking that some miraculous windfall

---

6   Trading Economics, 'United Kingdom Inflation Rate', https://tradingeconomics.com/united-kingdom/inflation-cpi, accessed 15 April 2025

will come along to relieve the situation. Living life that way means you are literally giving your own power away and crossing your fingers.

It does not have to be this way.

In order to have mental freedom, you must have a clear mind.

There are four important indicators that can be measured and improved and a five-step protocol to master the mind.

> **M** – Memory Baggage: Painful past events that carry an emotional charge
> **I** – Identity Clarity: Knowing exactly who you are, what you believe, and what your core values are.
> **N** – Narrative Ownership: Living based on your own values and not others' expectations or idealisms.
> **D** – Discernment: Questioning advice, culture, and norms before accepting them.

To improve Mental Freedom, you must use the CLEAR Protocol:

> **C** – Clarify identity and values
> **L** – Label past events neutrally
> **E** – Emotion regulation
> **A** – Audit influence
> **R** – Reflect daily

In this section of the book, I am going to show you how.

Watch your language

One of the best indicators of your current mindset, and one of the most important elements to be aware of when you're working to change it, is the language you use around your own beliefs. I'll unpick some of the most common beliefs we have around money in Part 2 and flip them on their head to show you how you can change them and in doing so, open yourself up to all the opportunities that surround you. For now, simply start to become aware of any negative beliefs you may hold. Bring them to the front of your awareness and actively challenge them.

Do you tell yourself that money is the root of all evil, or that money isn't important, or that all rich people rip others off? By being aware of these beliefs, you are taking the first step towards changing your mindset. What I want you to do as you read this book is to actively focus on reframing any negative beliefs that you uncover. In doing so, you will begin to move from a mindset of scarcity to one of abundance.

EXERCISE: Writing your money stories

This is a simple way to start identifying your beliefs around money to help you uncover the limiting ones you need to neutralise to put yourself in the right mindset to become free.

Simply complete the sentences below with what you truly believe at the moment (not what you think you should believe). You can also consider any other beliefs you have around money:

- Money is...
- If I became wealthy, it would mean...
- If I'm not financially independent, it's because...
- I'd love to have money, but...
- When I have money, I...
- Money doesn't...

Once you have identified some of the negative statements you tell yourself around money, you can reverse engineer them and tell yourself the opposite. In doing so, you will neutralise that limiting belief.

Identifying and neutralising your limiting beliefs surrounding money isn't about making those beliefs positive, but about injecting some positivity into your negative beliefs. This will allow you to find balance and realise that money is a neutral force in your life, not one that's weighted towards good or evil.

The flow of money

Money flows in all of our lives. It's not sexist, racist or biased in any way. When you understand this, you also realise you can take as much of it as you want. What stops money flowing in and out of your life in the way it should is your limiting beliefs. You have to dance with money, letting it in and out of your grip like a dance partner.

Any belief that stops this flow in your life will hold you back. For some people, it is the limiting belief that they aren't worthy of having money, so as soon as any comes into their possession, they spend it or give it away. For others it's the limiting belief that they have to struggle and grind for money, because that desperation to have money also pushes it away. Some people are so scared of losing money that they grip it too tightly, but this, too, stops the flow of money in their lives. They might not lose money, but nor do they attract any.

Money is the fairest game in town. This is one of the biggest mindset shifts you can have, and one that will make the greatest difference to your progress towards financial freedom.

When you develop an abundance mindset around money and are able to allow it to flow in and out of your life freely, you will become open to all manner of opportunities. Instead of dismissing things as too expensive or unaffordable, you will question why something has a high price tag, or why you might want to spend your money in one place over another. When you ask different questions, you receive different answers, and this in turn opens up a whole new world.

The biggest thing you will get from shifting your mindset to one of abundance is freedom of choice. What I share with you in this book isn't designed to change you as a person; in fact, it is designed to help you get closer to being who you really are. This will allow you to focus on what you love doing, naturally earn money by doing what you love and as a result, attract more of it into your life. It isn't only about being free in a financial sense, but also being free of the burden of other people's opinions, judgements and social ideals.

Identifying your vision

Parkinson's law states that if we had eight hours to do a specific task, we would fill all of that allowed time to complete the task.[7] However, if we had four hours to do the same task, we would most likely complete it in four hours. This indicates that we fill our time with stuff that is inefficient and not moving us towards our goals.

If we don't prioritise our time and our goals, we end up prioritising other people's goals. If we do not treat our goals like a doctor's appointment and put them in our calendar, we will find ourselves doing chores or running errands for other people. If we want a bigger life, we need a bigger vision for ourselves.

I would like you to complete an exercise and write out a vision for your ideal life.

---

7   Lark Editor Team, 'Parkinson's Law: A key to productivity' (Lark, 22 December 2023), www.larksuite.com/en_us/topics/productivity-glossary/parkinsons-law, accessed 15 October 2024

EXERCISE: What's your vision?

Spend some time writing down what your ideal life looks like. Imagine your perfect day and write that down too. Be as detailed and vivid as possible.

Think about these questions:

- What time would you wake up?
- Where would you wake up?
- Who would you be with?
- What view do you wake up to?
- What do you do first?
- Do you have breakfast?
- What do you have for breakfast?
- How do you spend the morning and afternoon?
- Where do you have dinner? What do you have for dinner?
- How do you spend the evening?

Get as clear as possible about what your perfect day would be, then make a commitment to live that day out twice per year as closely as you can. Put it in the diary and commit to it.

Once you have done it twice per year, try it monthly, then weekly.

What we practise, we get better at. This means you can manifest your ideal life quicker if you practise living it.

Look at your answers and ensure they are specific. Remember, your language dictates your actions and reality. It's important to reframe certain goals specifically because if you don't, not only will it make the goal harder to hit, but once you get close to it, you may end up being hesitant towards achieving it.

So many people tell me they want more time with their family without being specific on how much time they would actually like. If this resonates with you, imagine I granted your wish right now and said, 'I will give you £10 million and you can spend all your time with your family.' After a week or so, you might find that guilt creeps in because you realise you do *not* want to spend every minute with them. Who would? One of our most basic human needs is privacy, but because you haven't taken the time to set a specific goal, you may let that guilt convince you that allowing yourself privacy means you are a bad person.

A more realistic and specific goal might be 'I would love to be able to choose to spend x number of hours with my family at any given time to do y activities'. Although this might seem similar, it's actually a milestone you can measure and not feel guilty about because you'll achieve it.

Your language dictates your actions, so be specific with your language around goals.

Process over outcome

Before we go any further, we need to make sure you are able to attract money, accept money and use it as a tool. There can be absolutely nothing in the way that may limit or restrict that process.

You can whittle success down to the simple approach of short-term sacrifice for long-term achievement. People who have wild success in life are those who can do something today without seeing the result tomorrow. The world is owned by people who can keep focused on their goals without seeing a result immediately. They continue to do the necessary daily activities, knowing that just because they haven't seen a payoff today, doesn't mean they're never going to pay off. They know they will see the result next month or next year. The longer the time between when they do something and when they need to see the result, the bigger the result will be, and ultimately, the more successful they become.

Between 1968 and 1974, a series of delayed gratification experiments were carried out at Stanford University's Bing School using marshmallow and pretzel treats as rewards for children depending on their patience.[8] The children who waited for their treat

---

[8] T Watts, G Duncan and H Quan, 'Revisting the marshmallow test: A conceptual replication investigating links between early delay of gratification and later outcomes', *Psychological Science*, 29/7 (2018), 1159–1177, https://pmc.ncbi.nlm.nih.gov/articles/PMC6050075/#, accessed 31 January 2025

for fifteen minutes (only looking at it and not touching it) were allowed to eat it while the children who didn't make it to fifteen minutes (but held their treat during that time) were not permitted to eat it.

In 1990, the study was followed up during the kids' senior exams to determine if there was a direct correlation between those who were willing to delay gratification and success in their academia.[9] The results were staggering. Not only were the children who had waited for their treat more focused on their exams, the ongoing study also found that delayed gratification in childhood contributed towards their self-worth, self-esteem and ability to cope with stress in later life.

Your ability to delay gratification will unlock your potential to focus better, make progress faster and be significantly more conducive to your goal of becoming always free. Process over outcome is a concept I will delve into in more detail in Chapter 15.

TOP TIP

Being your true self gives you control and that, to me, is the ultimate freedom. While this book will share techniques to help you become financially free, growing your wealth is actually a side effect of identifying and following your purpose. What I would like you to do right now is accept that you are going to have money.

---

9   Ibid

PART 2
HOME TRUTHS

Make sure every action and decision aligns with who you truly are.

If you are to actually build the *Always Free* life you have in mind, it makes sense to question the people you are taking advice from to see if they have achieved the results you want. I'm not just referring to the actual advice, I'm talking about whether the strategy is even relevant anymore.

For example, did your parents tell you it was better to learn to drive a manual car instead of an automatic? Mine did. 'It will give you more options later,' they said. I was seventeen when I decided to learn to drive. At that particular time, automatic cars had been around for a while, but because both my mum and my step-dad had learned in a manual, they felt that it would be the better option for me, too.

As a result, I learned in a manual car, spent three times longer learning than I needed to, spent three times as much on lessons and tests, only to end up choosing to drive an automatic car.

Learning to drive in a manual car was good advice for my parents, but not for me. Not taking what you are told at face value and questioning everything you hear, regardless of the source, is a habit that will serve you well, and not only in relation to your journey towards financial freedom.

3
Question Everything

I have created a chart, shown below, that represents the inequitable distribution of the planet's wealth.

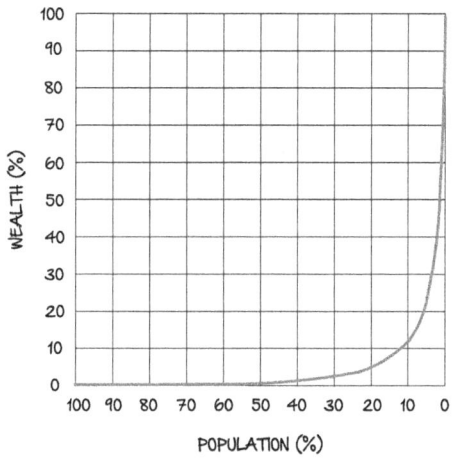

Wealth distribution chart

Approximately 1% of the world's population, comprising approximately 59.4 million individuals, holds about 45.8% of the world's total wealth. Collectively, the wealthiest 10% of the global population possess around 76% of global wealth.[10] You might find this fascinating, you might find it horrifying, but what does it have to do with financial freedom?

It's simple. If most of the world's population is getting it wrong when it comes to their finances, then it's safe to say that if you follow the strategies of the masses and take advice from most people, you won't end up where you want to be.

Let's take a look at some of the common strategies and beliefs that the majority of people submit to and see how they hold them back from designing the life they want. I'm going to flip these to show you what you should do instead. Think of this as an exercise in myth busting.

My aim here is to give you the truth so you then have the information to re-evaluate your own situation and ensure that the path you are currently on truly aligns with your core values. Here are my top pieces of advice in this area.

---

10 UBS, 'Global Wealth Report 2023' (15 August 2023), https://advisors.ubs.com/gaffneygroup/mediahandler/media/582898/global-wealth-report-2023.pdf, accessed 15 April 2025 and L Chancel et al, 'World Inequality Report 2022' (World Inequality Lab, 7 December 2021), https://wir2022.wid.world, accessed 16 April 2025

Don't respect your elders

This probably goes against everything you were told as a child, but look at the story about the way I was advised by my mum and step-dad to learn to drive a manual car because it had worked for them in an earlier age. There are many other strategies recommended to us that are not in our best interests today.

Advice from the previous generation is usually outdated. It's no longer relevant. Yes, of course there are universal principles that stand as true today as they did 6,000 years ago, but when it comes to financial freedom, unless you are taking advice from people who have truly achieved that, the information they impart is very likely to be useless.

Be careful who you choose to take advice from. You must learn to tune your radar sharply and recognise when you should take advice you're given with a pinch of salt (normally every time).

Challenge the status quo

Have you ever wondered why many of us associate watching TV with 'family time'?

If you check out the newspaper adverts from the 1950s, you will see that they displayed half-page images of smiling families gathered around the box. Captions from Motorola such as, 'TV helps your children at school' and 'TV adds so much to family happiness' were sprawled all over the newspapers to get people buying into the belief, creating a habit that would end up having the opposite effect.[11]

People who spend every night watching TV run the risk of being disconnected from their partners and children. However, nowadays, the majority of people still think that TV time is family time. If you are writing a blog or doing some research instead, you are considered to be ignoring the family and 'working' too much.

My point is, just because you have been told that watching TV is family time, it doesn't mean doing it will benefit any part of your life. It's simply what the manufacturers and their marketing teams wanted you to believe. It is a sales tactic that plays into the feelings of the consumer, and one that has been remarkably effective.

Here's another example of people not questioning the status quo, and when you look closely, it makes no sense at all. Have you ever wondered why people believe that they have to spend two months' salary on a diamond engagement ring to prove their love? Again, this belief is down to a marketing campaign, this time put together by the De Beer Diamond

---

11 LR Samuel, 'Brought to you by: Postwar television' (AEF, no date), https://aef.com/classroom-resources/book-excerpts/brought-postwar-television-advertising, accessed 15 April 2025

QUESTION EVERYTHING

Corporation.[12] Before the 1930s, people didn't have this belief. Now it's so deeply embedded in our culture that many people don't question it.

Diamonds are not even rare.[13] Their supply is deliberately controlled and campaigned in a way that makes us believe they are. Yet people still buy into this campaign today.

What can happen when you challenge the status quo?

Here's a story about a taxi driver who picked me up from my house a few years ago to take me to the airport. On the way, he explained that his goal was to work hard in two jobs until he could afford to own a house like mine, mortgage free.

I asked him what he planned to do once he reached that goal and I could tell from the change of expression on his face that he had never given that situation a single thought. While awaiting a reply, I explained that a house like that would be expensive to maintain and as I was talking, he had the dawning realisation

---

12 The Eye of Jewelry, 'De Beers' most famous ad campaign marked the entire diamond industry' (22 April 2020), https://theeyeofjewelry.com/de-beers/de-beers-jewelry/de-beers-most-famous-ad-campaign-marked-the-entire-diamond-industry, accessed 17 October 2024
13 A Briggs, 'Are diamonds rare? Debunking diamond myths' (VRAI, 10 October 2023), www.vrai.com/en-GB/journal/post/are-diamonds-rare, accessed 17 October 2024

that once he achieved his goal, he would likely have to continue working to support the house. He would not be free to enjoy himself. Is that a worthwhile goal?

I asked him how much equity he had in his house at that time and we calculated that if he just invested that equity at 8% per year, he would replace his income and not have to work at all. He would be financially free right then and there. His mind was blown.

The point is, people rarely take the time to question the status quo, do the maths, weigh up options with their own values and put a strategy in place to have it all. I'm going to give you that strategy.

Remember, freedom starts with having a free mind.

Everyone has an agenda

To master financial independence, you must first accept responsibility for your own actions going forward, and that means weighing up the reality of whether or not certain decisions have really given you the result you wanted. Have the actions you have taken based on what someone else has told you been aligned with your values? If not, did they give you the end result you wanted? I would guess they did not.

If you wanted to lose weight, would you take advice from a 25 stone man who spent all day in his bedroom playing computer games while eating pizza and drinking cola? Probably not.

If you wanted to improve your relationship with your partner or kids, would you take advice from someone who abandoned their kids while failing to keep their wedding vows and cheating on their partner? Probably not.

If you want a good result, do not take advice from someone with the opposite result to that which you are seeking. However, this is what many people do when it comes to lifestyle and wealth building without even knowing it. This is often caused by the manipulation of their beliefs by others and their own lack of simply questioning the injected opinions and views.

Whenever people give you advice, remember it's based around their own values, experiences, perceptions and achievements in life. What worked or didn't work for them is not usually what will or won't work for you.

TOP TIP

To start taking control, you must first learn to question what you have been told so far and everything going forward. Form your own opinions and synthesise paradoxes based on other people's values.

What people tell you is usually based on what will serve *them* best, not you.

4
Money Myths

You may have heard financial gurus say that you should save 10% of your income. Personally, I find this is an incomplete strategy that can leave you disempowered and deflated when you realise where it gets you.

For the record, I am not saying saving is a bad idea, but if you save 10% of your income for ten years, you will have one year's worth of income saved. Most people work for forty to forty-five years, so if you save for forty-five years, you will have just 4.5 years' worth of income when you stop working.

After working for all that time, possibly in a job you didn't care very much about, you can afford to live for 4.5 years on your savings. If you retire at sixty-five, you'd better hope that you don't live beyond sixty-nine, because you will have more life at the end of your money than money at the end of your life. Not to mention inflation, the extra time you will have to spend, treats for the grandkids etc. If all you did was follow this strategy, you would likely end up with about six months' worth of money (over and above any state, company or private pension you're entitled to) to sustain your lifestyle.

There are methods of savings that I absolutely promote and recommend, and I will cover these in this book, but my point here is to follow the advice in Chapter 3 and question the reality of the strategies you hear from people. Do the maths because, just like the pension trap or the taxi driver's big mortgage-free house, sometimes it's not the full picture.

Money is time

Growing up, I was always led to believe that time is money. The neighbours on my estate would tell me this, my bosses would tell me this, my colleagues would tell me this and my family would say the same.

When I was thirteen years old, I realised that time is only money if money is all you want. If you want money and you are paid an hourly rate, you can provide your service for an hour and get paid an hour's worth of money, but there are a few fundamental flaws with the scalability of this behaviour:

- Your earning ability is limited by the number of hours in the day.

- The more money you want to earn, the more you have to work.

- There is a point at which your hourly rate demands more responsibility, pressure and sacrifice to your wellbeing than you are willing and able to give.

As a result, you become frustrated, tired, resentful and unfulfilled, which limits you from sustaining this approach. For years, I subscribed to the idea that there is a direct correlation between time and money, but all this did was make it extremely difficult to break out of the societal comfort zone and start designing my life how I wanted it to be.

If you think that time is equal to money, that means you associate working more hours with being paid more, and for most people, that results in working themselves into the ground with absolutely no free time. They become unhappy because they feel unfulfilled or unrewarded.

There is a simple way to know if you are trading time for money. If you feel resentful at any point in your business or job, the chances are you have crossed the subconscious barrier of self-worth and you are thinking, 'I shouldn't be doing this.' If you ever find yourself in this situation, you are trading higher-value time for lower-value money.

If people feel like this every day in their job or business, without knowing it, they are forcing themselves into a state of mind that craves escape. They count down the days to time off. They wait all year for their annual holiday, praying for it to hurry up. They watch the clock until Friday, and when it comes, they fuel the feeling of escapism by spending everything they earned that week on quick-fix luxuries during their time away from work.

If you feel like you have reached the point where you find yourself resenting working too much, it means that you value your time more than you value the money you are earning. What does this mean? It means what you are actually working for is to have more free time, but the belief that time is money is actually restricting you from having that time because there is a conflict.

You must work more to get more money and the money you get will allow you to have more time, right?

Wrong!

All this does is put you on an endless treadmill of hard work, pressure, stress, no free time and usually much frustration. Whether you like to acknowledge it or not, we all have a threshold inside of us that, if crossed, turns us from being happy to being resentful. It's an internal threshold that can only be appreciated when it's tested, but we all have it.

For me now, money is time.

Time is your most valuable asset

My wife Sarah loves animals. She is also one of the most altruistic people I know. She tends to put other people first and finds it very difficult to say no (although she is working on it).

One weekend, Sarah decided that she would like to do something to keep her active and earn a bit of income on the side. We spoke about it for a while and agreed that dog walking would be perfect. It would be a way to do something she loves while keeping fit and gaining some extra money. If any dog owner could describe the ideal person to take care of their beloved dog, it would be Sarah.

We sat down and designed the model, the services and how it would all work, factoring in whether the clients had big dogs or small dogs, whether they wanted their dog walked on its own or with others etc. Sarah was excited to start and because working with dogs required no motivation, it didn't feel like a job… until it did.

Before we could let everyone know about the structured pricing, word had already got round and Sarah had accepted a few clients and given them an hourly rate. I explained that no matter how much you love something or how much you think you could do it for free, if you exceed your internal self-worth, you will start to resent what you are doing. This is why it would have been wise to start her venture once the outcome-based pricing was set up instead of providing services with time-based pricing.

Nonetheless, at first, Sarah was energised. She grew fond of the dogs, kept fit walking them each day and was able to generate the bit of extra income she craved. Then one afternoon, I got a call.

'I can't believe the clients have gone out and now I'm having to wait for them to get back before I can leave.'

A couple had let Sarah take their dog for a walk and then gone out for an hour, meaning that Sarah had to wait for their return because the dog could not be left alone.

The threshold of Sarah's internal self-worth was being tested. Without realising it, she had discovered how much her time was worth and at this point, it became more valuable than the money she was charging. Her attitude changed from appreciation to resentment. It didn't matter that the couple would have happily paid Sarah extra for staying late, her time was more valuable than the fair exchange she had charged.

That night, Sarah told me she realised that the most valuable thing to us is our time. No matter what we do or how much we love doing it, time will always be our most valuable asset.

Understanding your time-value threshold

It's difficult to know your time-value threshold without being in a situation like Sarah's. The chances are you have experienced something similar once or twice in your life already. You have probably complained to your partner about your boss expecting you to do something or bitched about someone keeping you waiting for a meeting. It's these situations that highlight your value on time.

If you can learn to identify what you value your time at before it reaches the threshold, you stand the best chance of never putting yourself in a situation that exceeds it.

Self-worth

If you have ever felt undervalued, it is because you believed you got an unfair deal based on the value you provided compared to the reward you received. Take mental notes when those moments happen and protect your value at all costs.

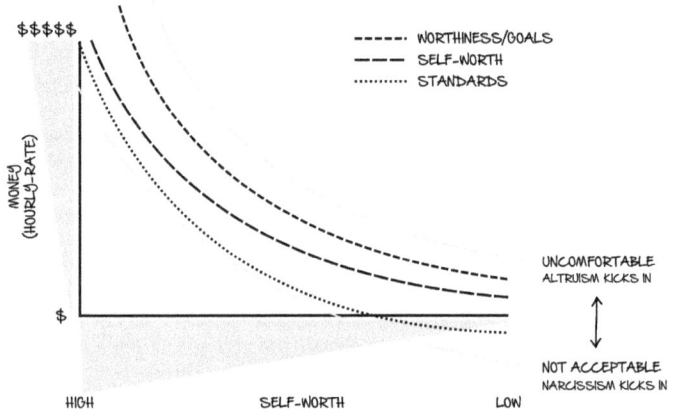

Self-worth chart

Your self-worth sits somewhere between two internal thresholds. The upper threshold is the limit to which you believe you are worth. Receiving anything above this level will feel uncomfortable and you will start to become overly altruistic and giving.

The lower threshold is your standards. Every time you drop below your standards, you won't accept it and as a result, you will become slightly more narcissistic.

The lower your self-worth, the smaller your goals and the less money you are willing to accept. The higher your self-worth, the bigger your goals and the more money you are willing to accept. It's all about how you value yourself and your time.

How do you put a value on time? First of all, you must shift your thinking from 'time is money' to 'money is time'. Think in terms of how money can provide you with the time you need instead of how much time you need to sacrifice to get x amount of money.

I'm going to show you exactly how much your time costs shortly, but before I do, you must first appreciate that money will play a role. It's not so much how much you earn but what you do with it. Wealth and financial freedom have nothing to do with how much money you earn, but everything to do with how you manage what you earn.

TOP TIP
Value your time more than you value your money and you will end up with plenty of both.

5
Net Worth Is Not Wealth

'The more I am worth, the wealthier I will be.' Really?

One belief I encounter time and again is that people would be happier and wealthier if they had more money. I'm here to tell you that is not the case.

Many people I talk to (like the taxi driver) tell me that their goal is to be worth a certain amount of money, as if that will make *the* difference to their life. If they could just be a millionaire, their problems would go away, and because of what they have heard, they measure wealth using net worth. It's not hard to see why, when magazines like *Forbes* have a 'rich list' based on net worth.

Although tracking your net worth is a sensible thing to do when you're building wealth, it certainly will not be your door to freedom. It's important to reset your way of thinking about the relationship between money, wealth and freedom because, as I said before, continuing through life with a belief that has been passed on to you by peers and society can seriously ruin your chance of obtaining any freedom at all.

If there is one thing that stands out to me when I think of the most common misconceptions about money, it's that the majority of people think that if you are a millionaire, you can afford anything. There is a warped perception that if you are a millionaire, you must be wealthy, but wealth has nothing to do with being a millionaire.

What are your goals?

When you ask someone what their goals are, many will say, 'One day I'm going to be a millionaire,' like it's an overnight transformation in their life. This goal is usually high on the priority list as it's perceived as the end game. People think that if they become a millionaire, their money problems are over.

If you were to ask them to be more specific and state how much money they want exactly, they might sit and think about it for a minute before coming up with a random rounded number. There is no maths, no number crunching; they just reply with something like, 'I want to have a net worth of £2 million.' They might explain, '£2 million is an amount that will allow me to afford anything I want.' The problem with this way of thinking is that no matter how much money they have upwards of £1 million, they will never actually be wealthy because of their misconstrued perception and their lack of understanding of wealth.

Wealth is not correlated to how much money you earn or accumulate.

There are a number of reasons why this is a common trap. Let's take a young enthusiastic entrepreneur who wants to become a millionaire and accumulate a net worth of £2 million.

Imagine I said to them, 'I will get you a net worth of £2 million by going out and acquiring for you ten properties worth £500,000 each.' With a portfolio of ten properties each worth £500,000, the entrepreneur is controlling £5 million worth of property.

However, to control that much property, of course they will have some debt in the form of mortgage loans. Let's say the debt is £3 million, so:

Non-liquid assets in the form of houses = £5,000,000
− Debt/liabilities/loans/mortgages = £3,000,000
= Entrepreneur's net worth = £2,000,000

At that point, the entrepreneur has reached their goal of becoming a millionaire and accumulating a net worth of £2 million. On paper, they have achieved their dream.

Have they really, though?

The thing to pay attention to here is the debt. If the interest rate on the mortgages is 5% per year and the debt is £3,000,000, then the interest repayments are £150,000 alone. That's £12,500 per month.

On top of this, there will be some maintenance costs associated with the properties. For this example, let's estimate these to be £10,000 per year, per property. That's another £100,000 per year on top of the £150,000, so we now have a total of £250,000 per year in costs.

Let's say that there is a dip in the rental market due to there being more houses available than people who want to rent. In this example, we'll say that out of the ten houses, only five of them are currently being rented for £2,000 per month each.

Five properties at £2,000 per month is a total of £10,000 per month, or £120,000 per year, in income. The entrepreneur is spending £250,000 per year in running costs. The running costs minus the rental income equates to a shortfall of £130,000 per year. That's £10,833.33 per month.

Our entrepreneur friend who set out to have a net worth of £2 million has achieved their goal, but they are haemorrhaging £10,833.33 per month. They have what they wanted, but they are seriously stressed out and broke.

Millionaires can still have money worries

You can be a broke millionaire. Most are equity millionaires, meaning their net worth is tied up in non-liquid assets.[14]

The millionaire in my example now has to afford to run their properties by going out and finding enough money to cover the rent until they become occupied, or they need to get rid of the properties by selling them, but if no one is renting, the chances are no one is buying either. They feel trapped.

Because they didn't crunch their numbers, they have failed to create any financial independence and have instead created the opposite. They must work longer and harder, giving them less free time.

---

14 A Wolfson, 'Rich people are now keeping about 1/4 of their money in this asset class, survey finds. But is it right for you?' (Market Watch, 17 June 2023), www.marketwatch.com/picks/rich-people-are-now-keeping-about-1-4-of-their-money-in-this-asset-class-survey-finds-but-is-it-right-for-you-a7061b6d, accessed 15 April 2025

This could have been avoided if the entrepreneur had focused on how the money was spent rather than how much money they could obtain.

I see similar situations in relation to property all the time, where people think that getting on the property ladder will help them become financially free. Buying a house to live in has literally nothing to do with financial freedom. It actually moves you further away from it.

The objectives for financial freedom are to increase your liquid assets, control or reduce your lifestyle costs within your means, and develop leveraged income streams. A property that you live in yourself will decrease your liquid assets, increase your lifestyle costs and will not generate leveraged income.

You need cash to pay for your lifestyle. If you freeze the tap you drink from, you have to find more water from somewhere else.

Becoming a millionaire is not necessarily as life changing as some people think if the wealth isn't managed wisely. When you calculate your net worth figure and realise that you are a millionaire on paper, nothing changes in your life, trust me. You get up, you do the same routine and nothing looks different.

Why doesn't it change anything? Because it's just a figure relative to your lifestyle. You can still be stressed, resentful and extremely unhappy.

NET WORTH IS NOT WEALTH

The millionaire and the paperboy

One evening, my son Harrison told me that he would love to save up to buy himself a games console. We had recently moved into a new house and there were plenty of chores that needed doing, so he came to me and asked if he could help with the chores in return for some pocket money each week. I told him that he could work on weekends when he wasn't at school and he committed to it.

We sat down and worked out how long each task would take, how much Sarah and I would pay him for each task and how long it would be before he could afford to buy his games console. Over the coming weeks, he helped unbox our possessions, jet hose the patio, clear the gutters, clean the greenhouse and wash the windows.

As the weeks went on and we approached the halfway mark, my son asked if he could use some of the money he had earned to buy some football stickers and a sticker album. He explained that his friend had a paper round and he was buying the new football sticker album at the end of the week when he got paid.

Harrison was keen to buy the sticker album until I explained to him that it would delay the purchase of his games console. If he was to take some of the money he had saved to buy the football stickers and sticker album, he would have to work for another week and a half and wait another two weeks to get the console.

His reply was, 'I wish I earned more money because then I could buy what I like.'

The following weekend, once my son had finished his chores, his friend with the paper round came over for dinner. As he arrived, I answered the door and greeted him by saying, 'Ah, money bags is here!' My son stood at the door cringing as I continued, 'I hear you bought that new sticker album.'

My son's friend smiled as he whipped it out of his bag, desperate to show us. He said, 'I'm going to complete the collection before anyone else!' I could tell my son was slightly envious of the sticker album as he watched his friend frantically flicking through the pages, showing me his special shiny stickers.

'How much is a pack of stickers?' I asked the lad as he stuffed the book back into his rucksack.

'£2 each pack,' he replied. 'And I get paid £11 per week so I'm going to buy five packs every Friday,' he added.

'Oh cool,' I said. 'How is the paper round going? Are you enjoying it?'

He replied, 'Yeah, it's not bad. I wish they paid me a bit more, though, so I could afford more stickers because I want to be the first to complete the collection.'

The boy was earning £11 per week and spending £10 per week on stickers, which left him with £4 for the month. He told me he would then spend £1 per week on sweets. My son told me that the boy didn't even like football and was just trying to complete the sticker album first to show off to his friends at school. He was yearning for more money to buy more stickers he didn't really want while keeping just enough to pay for his sweet expenses.

That evening, once the boy had left, I asked my son, 'You know when you said that if you earned more money, you could buy what you like?'

'Yes,' he said.

'Well, most highly paid people are no better off than your friend. They can have all the money in the world and still not be happy.'

At the time, our next-door neighbour was earning £20,800 post-tax income per month. While I was in conversation with him one day, he told me how stressed he was with his current situation. Intoxicated with alcohol, he poured his heart out, explaining that he was losing the will to live.

'I don't know what's going wrong,' he said, then he proceeded to tell me about his three cars, two health club memberships, his team of gardeners, nannies, yacht storage and mooring costs. This guy was spending just over £19,000 per month on his lifestyle. Despite having £1,500 left over as 'disposable' income at the end of each month, he was on medication for high blood pressure and his wife was about to leave him. He had no savings or liquidity.

After doing some quick maths, I calculated that if he lost his income tomorrow, he would only have enough cash to cover one month's worth of expenses before he would radically have to change his lifestyle and start selling off his possessions. He was no better off in terms of prosperity than the paperboy; in fact, he was worse off.

I scribbled down some maths for my son to show him the correlation between the two situations:

Paperboy:
Active income per month: £44
Expenses per month: £40
Disposable income: £4
Time working per month: 8 hours
$44 \div 40 = 1.1$ months of wealth

High-earning neighbour:
Active income per month: £20,800
Expenses per month: £19,300

Disposable income: £1,500
Time working per month: 80 hours
20,800 ÷ 19,300 = 1.08 months of wealth

We found that actually, the neighbour was working ten times longer and had far more stress than the paperboy. He was on a hamster wheel of death.

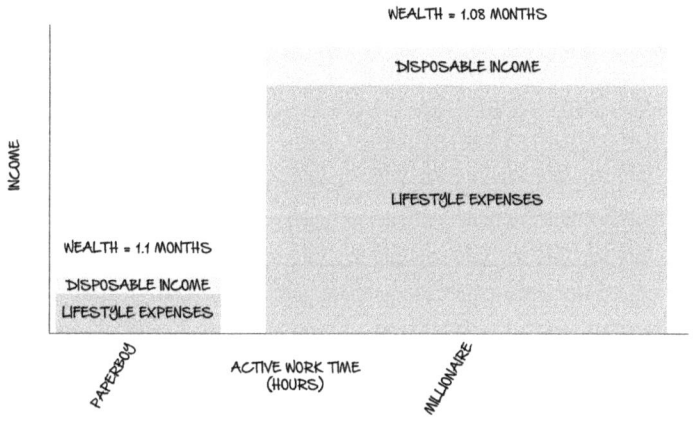

Lifestyle expenses and disposable income

I explained to my son that his friend spending around 90% of his income on things he doesn't really like to impress other people wasn't that different to most of the working population. Most people have less than 9.9% of their income left each and every month and no matter how many pay rises they get, the same ratio will apply.[15]

---

15 D Milliken, 'Four years after pandemic shock, UK household saving stays high', Reuters (22 July 2024), www.reuters.com/world/uk/four-years-after-pandemic-shock-uk-household-saving-stays-high-2024-07-22, accessed 15 April 2025

Wealth, freedom and prosperity have nothing to do with how much you earn. They have everything to do with how you manage what you earn. Being a millionaire simply isn't life changing. What is life changing is the day you never have to set an alarm clock or answer to anyone. The day you get to choose how you spend your time.

Truly financially free millionaires usually have very little in their bank account because their money is all being used to generate leveraged income to pay for their lifestyle. I'll show you how to do this later.

TOP TIP
Time is your most valuable asset. Time must always be the objective because that is what everyone yearns for more than anything else. If you are to build wealth and financial freedom, you must build it with the right objective.

6
Look Within

The next truth I want to share with you is that nothing you buy, no one you meet and no amount of money will result in your happiness.

You won't find happiness by looking for it. Whenever I hear people speaking about happiness or purpose, they usually refer to it as an external thing they are on the search for. Happiness is not something you find and purpose is not something you stumble upon.

Although your dreams, goals and destiny are things you are moving towards and are in the future, your purpose is inside of you already. It's been there from the moment you were born and is demonstrated by your daily actions.

There will be certain moments of inspiration that make you who you are. These occur when you are living congruently to your highest values. It's wise to understand that if you have things you are being called towards, yet you are only feeling moments of inspiration at certain times, it's because your actions are out of alignment with your values.

Freedom is a choice. Happiness is being in control of what you do. It's choosing the way you spend your time, who you spend it with and how you live. You are most happy when you are simply being you.

We make around 35,000 decisions every day.[16] That's over 127,000,000 decisions every decade. Each decision we have ever made has ultimately led us to where we are right now, so if we have a natural inner desire guiding us towards our most inspired lives, why is it that sometimes we feel we are off track from where we thought we would be?

If you are not where you want to be right now, it is likely to be for one or both of these reasons:

- You are trying to achieve something that isn't truly important to you and may be looking up to someone else with a particular set of results.

---

16 EM Krockow, 'How many decisions do we make each day?' *Psychology Today* (27 September 2018), www.psychologytoday.com/gb/blog/stretching-theory/201809/how-many-decisions-do-we-make-each-day, accessed 17 October 2024

- Your daily decisions have been influenced by fears caused by the opinions of others, the injection of their values or listening to poor advice and taking on board outdated strategies from those who have not achieved the results you are after.

This is your life. Believe in yourself. Take control of your life and give yourself permission to be more who you want to be with absolutely no conditions. Be happy now.

People do not want you to succeed

The chances are, at some point in your life, you have gone after something and as you started striving towards it, some of the people around you, maybe your social group or family, told you to slow down. Have you ever thought that's a bit weird? I did.

I found that the more focused I became in achieving my goals, the more distractions there would be from others. People would tell me I was putting too much pressure on myself.

The thing is, human beings are hard wired for survival of the fittest. Whenever you are striving for greatness in any area of your life, you are essentially increasing your chances of surviving longer. At an evolutionary level, other human beings will then start to see you as a threat. They will also feel uncomfortable and inferior to you when you cross a threshold where they perceive you to be 'better' than them.

A common example is when people decide to lose weight and get in shape. At first, their friends seem supportive and encourage them to pursue the goal.

As the weight starts to come off and they get in better shape, though, the friends' comments turn to ones like, 'I think you are going too far now' or 'Don't lose any more weight, you are too slim'. The friends who are making those comments are overlooking the fact that the person losing weight and getting in shape might not yet be at their desired goal. Eventually, when the threat is too much, some 'friends' may even turn away and talk about them behind their back.

When you strive to be better, most of the people around you will be happy for you and seem supportive up until the point where they perceive that you're doing better than they are in a particular area. It's an instinct of survival. You have unrooted something inside of them that they're not happy with, so they will secretly want you to fail.

I often receive messages from people telling me they would love to do this or that, but are afraid of what Mum and Dad will say or that their friends won't support them. If you are waiting for everyone's approval all the time, you are holding back your own success.

Don't let people's negativity towards your goals dishearten or stop you.

The pursuit of financial freedom and living your best life will take courage. Don't expect everyone to understand you and certainly don't expect support. You will be going against other people's opinions, advice, feelings, strategies, beliefs and ideals.

Conformity is simply living your life by rules that have been made up by others. Create your own rules. Live by them.

My lightbulb moments

When I was thirteen years old, I had two realisations that changed the way I thought and radically shifted my path in life. Had I not spent time around so many different people, these realisations may not have manifested.

Growing up on an estate, I met people from all walks of life, old and young; there were people with drug problems, people on benefits, people who had jobs, and there were single parents. No matter what their situation, they all always had problems with money.

I know this because every Friday evening, a crowd used to congregate at the foot of my block and sit on the steps, talking about how money was the root of all evil. They would comment on how bad their week had been and often refer to their bosses or wealthy people as greedy, saying things like, 'Why can't they just give me some of their money if they have so much of it? They won't miss it.'

I would pick up on these conversations and question the conflicting views going on. One minute, they were saying money is evil, the next minute they wanted rich people to give them some money. I didn't really understand what the issue was, but I certainly knew something wasn't quite right and wondered if the problem lay in the people rather than money.

The funny thing was that, after spending an hour talking about their disgust towards money, at six-thirty, they would hand their change over to a guy so he could go and buy a syndicate ticket for the weekly lottery. For the next half hour, the conversation would shift to what they would do with the money if they won and how great their lives would be.

I was confused. Why would they yearn to win something they considered to be evil? Although I didn't have all the answers, I felt like I could see something they couldn't.

In April that same year, I set my heart on owning a BMX bike. My birthday was in October, so I thought six months was enough time to drop hints to my mum and step-dad that I would love the bike as a present.

I absolutely fell in love with a Chrome Mongoose Sniper for sale at £200 in a local bike shop. I asked the shop owner if I could take the catalogue away so I could get a photocopy, then I spent my pocket money on ten blown-up pictures of the bike. That night, I stuck those pictures everywhere: in my room, under my parents' pillow, in the food cupboard, in the toilet.

My parents got the hint, but told me that they wouldn't be able to afford £200. They did, however, offer me a deal. If I could raise £100, they would pay the other £100. I had no idea how I was going to earn £100, but I shook on the deal and the next day I got to work.

On the estate where I lived, there were triangular greens in the middle of each group of three blocks of flats. The residents would park their cars around these greens. The most obvious thing for me to do to start earning my £100 was to wash these cars. It was spring, the days were getting longer and the timing was ideal.

I filled up a bucket with water and put some soap in it, grabbed a sponge and cloth, and then spent about two hours plucking up the courage to knock on doors and ask if anyone would like their car washed. The only car I washed on the first day was a white Volkswagen Golf. I spent hours on it. I wanted it to be pristine so there was no possibility of the owner being unhappy with my job. As it was getting dark, I asked for the £5 fee and after she'd looked round the car, the owner gave me that plus a £2 tip. I was delighted.

That evening, my friend came over. I explained to him about my mission to raise money for my bike and how the car wash was going to help me get there. He offered to help the next day, but I declined, saying that I only had one bucket and sponge (I didn't like to tell him that I wanted the money for myself to get it saved for the bike quicker).

At that moment, my step-dad came into my room and asked me if I would like anything from the supermarket as he was going to get some shopping. I'm not sure what came over me, but something made me give him everything I had earned that day so he could buy me another bucket and sponge for my friend.

The next day, something remarkable happened. My friend and I washed four cars. The day after that, we washed six cars. Then, as the weeks passed, more of our friends wanted to help us and cut in on the deal. They would use their own buckets and sponges so I didn't have to spend more of my earnings, and by the end of the summer, we were a team of five. We were washing more than twenty-five cars per week over a two-week period, and then starting the cycle all over again every fortnight. It was amazing.

The best bit was that I was no longer washing cars. Instead, I was knocking on the doors, booking in customers and collecting money. I was getting paid the most money for doing the least work.

This was the moment when I had the realisation that money isn't evil at all. I realised that if you use and invest money in the right way, it can actually be liberating. Time isn't money; money is time.

At the age of thirteen, I realised that wherever you go, whatever you do, if you treat money the wrong way, the same problems will follow you around. However, if you use it the right way, you can do more of what you want to do and have the experiences you want in life.

I learned a valuable lesson that shaped my life from that point on, and that was if you value your time and enjoyment more than you value money, you end up with plenty of both.

I picked my BMX up just as the bike shop opened on 20 October 1995 and I will never forget the appreciation I had for that moment. Not just the bike itself, but for the way I had used leverage to pay for my half of the deal.

It's all about you

With finances, wealth and prosperity, most people are unaware of the habits and traps that stop them from accumulating any. They may think it's an external problem, but it's not. To master this area of our life, we must first understand that we are in control, nobody else.

I want to encourage you to accept 100% ownership and responsibility for your situation now. If you do so, you will find you open up more opportunities, you'll have more clarity and you will certainly attract more wealth and success as you watch your life transform before your eyes.

The smell under your nose

We are about to start mapping out a strategy for your financial freedom. The turning point in your financial destiny starts with you, but the hardest part of having a problem is admitting you are the problem.

Hopefully you have already had some mindset shifts in terms of financial freedom, but I still need to say one last thing before we get stuck into the good stuff:

If you are the problem, admit it. Own it.

Have you ever unknowingly trodden in dog poo and walked around with the unmistakable pong wafting past your nose every now and then? At first, you think it's the place you are in, so you move away, but realise it also smells bad where you've moved to. You might ask someone if they can smell it too. When they say no, you move again. This goes on until you check your shoe and find that the smell under your nose is following you around because it's on you!

LOOK WITHIN

The first thing you need to do to move forward in your financial independence journey is to identify any bad smells you are carrying around from place to place and get rid of them.

Your beliefs are your choice. Everything you achieve in life starts with a choice.

TOP TIP

Happiness is having the choice to spend your time how you wish. Happiness is also an ongoing pursuit as your life changes. The moment you understand this, you can embrace happiness and appreciate the journey instead of thinking of happiness as a place you reach and stop.

PART 3
A GLIMPSE OF REALITY

Managing your finances enables you to build a life around what you are inspired to do and so become a better human being.

Now that I have shared some misconceptions, traps and myths about financial freedom, it's only right that I share some insights that I have learned on my own path. I hope you take these insights on board and save yourself a lot of time on your own journey to becoming *Always Free*.

These are epiphanies that have allowed me to stay focused on my wealth building and achieve success:

- Self-worth is where it all starts.

- Self-worth is directly correlated to your net worth and your probability of living an extraordinary life.

- Many people just don't feel worthy of building wealth and a life they want.

In this part, we will look more deeply into the subject of self-worth, then go on to discuss how you can take control of your life and design your route to financial freedom.

7
Exploring Your Self-Worth

As I've already said, the purpose of this book is not to make you a new person, but to get you back to being who you truly want to be. To get to that point, you must embrace the fact that your self-worth dictates your standards of life. It's much easier and more effortless to build wealth when you are being yourself and loving who you are.

Imitation is self-worth suicide because you are hiding yourself to be someone else. The reason for this is that you have a low self-worth.

Having a low self-worth can affect many areas of your life including relationships, health, your business and building wealth. People with a low self-worth have different beliefs to people with a high self-worth and they often speak with a negative language pattern about themselves. People with a high self-worth believe they can be, do and have anything they set their mind to.

You will never be financially free if you have a low self-worth and a desire to please, appease and impress other people. To build an extraordinarily wealthy life, you must raise your worthiness and believe you are destined for greatness.

In 1895, historian Hubert Howe Bancroft published his lifelong research in *The Book of Wealth*.[17] Only 400 copies were ever published and they were distributed to the wealthiest families on the planet. The ten-volume set of books was described by Bancroft as 'An inquiry into the nature and distribution of the world's resources and riches, and a history of the origin and influence of property, its possession, accumulation and disposition in all ages and among all nations.' It was a study of what contributed to forming the greatest and wealthiest people on the planet over the last 6,500 years.

In summary, the books describe a few common traits of the most successful people in history. The conclusion is closely linked to axiology, which is a study of values and worth. Every successful person who has managed to build a vast fortune has believed that they

---

17   H Bancroft, *The Book of Wealth*, www.thebookofwealth.org, accessed 16 October 2024

were worthy of receiving it in the first place. They had a high self-worth, placed a high value on serving great numbers of people and as a result, generated a high net worth.

People who place value on serving others but have a low self-worth do not become wealthy. People who have a high self-worth but place a low value on serving others do not become wealthy. Self-worth together with valuing serving others is directly correlated to the net worth of an individual. The way to raise your self-worth in the first place is to have a purpose to build both that and your service to others.

Bearing all of that in mind, and given the importance of developing your self-worth to your journey to financial freedom, we are now going to explore that very subject. Be honest, be open and be ready to start making meaningful changes in your life.

Know your purpose and structure your life around it

If you wake up in the morning and you don't know what you want to do with your life, you feel as if your life has no meaning, then you'll feel like you're constantly on a treadmill going through the motions every day. You will be living for pleasure and trying to avoid pain, and as a result have a low self-worth.

Usually, a low self-worth is the result of guilt, shame or unrealistic expectations to live and excel outside of your values. Often this stems from ideas forced on you by peers, parents or society. It's also important to know that the more you judge others in the outer world, the more you will judge yourself internally. If you want to start controlling your destiny, you must stop subordinating yourself to other people's opinions and values.

If you have guilt or shame from the past, it's important to take some time to ask yourself what action or trait you specifically feel guilty about. Then write down a list of 100 ways in which those actions or traits have benefited or served you well to this day. For example, if you were mean to someone in your younger years, that may have led to you being more empathetic and compassionate since then. List all the events that evidence this. If you tend to be impatient, that may encourage you to get on with what needs to be done rather than procrastinating.

The entire time you carry guilt, you will struggle to find your purpose. You are then unlikely to want to serve other people, and you certainly will not feel worthy of receiving money and building wealth.

When you find out what is truly meaningful to you and build a life around it, you set goals that are inspiring to you. When you set goals that inspire you, you achieve them and feel accomplished, which builds momentum and ever greater degrees of self-worth.

Stop looking up to people

Looking up to people causes you to lower your self-worth. People who haven't given themselves permission to figure out their true purpose live in the expectations and shadows of others and beat themselves up when they don't achieve unrealistic goals that are not aligned with their values.

If your parents wanted and expected you to be a doctor, even though they weren't doctors and it was never what you wanted for yourself, why lower your self-worth by worrying about not having appeased them? All you will do is beat yourself up, belittle yourself and feel unmotivated and unaccomplished.

Give yourself permission to grow in your own direction. No one ever wakes up in the morning and says, 'I want less money by this time tomorrow.' Deep down, we all want to grow, but at the surface level, many of us have injected limiting, restricting and fearful beliefs and taboos about what it means to expand. Therefore, we struggle to make our dreams a reality.

You cannot give without taking. You cannot take without giving. Life is a game of fair exchange.

Your values dictate your financial destiny

It's fair to say that we are exposed to plenty of wealth strategies in our lifetimes. We are inundated with the next big methods of making money or achieving financial freedom. You may have already tried your hand at one or more of these strategies.

There are lots of strategies, but few results. Only a tiny percentage of people have success. Why?

Usually what happens is people try their hand at something, and then resent their situation even more because the strategy doesn't meet their expectations. They don't get the result they thought they would, they get discouraged and become deflated.

If you think you don't get results because you are too young, remember Mark Zuckerberg was nineteen when he started coding Facebook.[18] If you think it's because you are too old, Colonel Sanders was sixty-five when he started KFC.[19] If you think you are too busy, I was running a business with seventeen staff and raising two kids under nine years old when I became financially free.

---

18 The Information Architects of the Encyclopaedia Britannica, 'Mark Zuckerberg: Facts and related content' (Britannica), www.britannica.com/facts/Mark-Zuckerberg, accessed 17 October 2024

19 University of Houston, Colonel Harland Sanders (Conrad N Hilton College of Global Hospitality Leadership), https://uh.edu/hilton-college/About/Hospitality-Industry-Hall-of-Honor/Inductees/Colonel-Harland-Sanders%20/#, accessed 17 October 2024

You might say, 'Well, I'm learning now' and that's fine, but understand that it has always been possible for you to achieve this goal; it's just that until now, you haven't had it high enough in your values. The truth is, unless you have a real burning desire to build wealth and achieve financial freedom, the likelihood of it happening is small.

If you are not as wealthy as you would like to be yet, you haven't valued getting there as much as you have valued other things in your life to this point. If you haven't achieved financial freedom yet, this means it hasn't been high enough on your values list until now. Simple.

What do you value?

Everyone has their own set of values, ranging from what they value most to what they value least. Everyone also finds wealth in what they value most, just not always in cash form.

Some people value family and are extremely good when it comes to raising kids, dealing with siblings and looking after the home. People who don't value family as much are not so good at these things, so they pay for others to do them (school teachers, housekeepers, au pairs etc).

Some people value great health and vitality. They spend time preparing nutritious meals, drinking water and exercising regularly. People who don't value these things so much pay others to help or support them (personal trainers, chefs, gyms etc).

Some people value a wealth of knowledge in a certain subject and are great teachers. Others are willing to pay to learn from these teachers.

Whatever's highest on your list of values is what you are inspired from within to fulfil. You have wealth in this area, which is the one you are most organised, reliable and disciplined in. In the same way, whatever you prioritise least, you are forgetful in, you are unorganised with, you need reminding to do it and have few results to show for it.

When you walk down the street, what do you spot in the environment? Do you see:

- Family stores?
- Shoe shops?
- Technology shops?
- Health and fitness shops?
- Music shops?

Whatever you value most, you will see in your environment. You will bring it up in conversation and you will be known for talking about it knowledgeably. There will be certain things that you have fantastic memory retention in and others you forget almost as quickly as you become aware of them.

For anyone to achieve financial freedom, they must first have it high on their values, and then build it in a way that doesn't require them to live outside of their other high values. If you are a vegan and love animals, it will be almost impossible for you to build wealth and achieve financial freedom by running a slaughterhouse. If you love eating healthy foods and value your personal fitness, you will have a hard time trying to reach financial independence working in fast food. See where I am going with this?

This is what people do when they attempt to mimic many of the wealth gurus out there. They get infatuated with a result that has been achieved by someone with a completely different value system.

Not only are they trying to replicate something that isn't aligned with their true values, they are also usually only seeing one piece of the puzzle. It's not just information that stops us building wealth, it's the fact we don't know how to act on that information and build a synthesised strategy that supports our value system. Not doing this is a recipe for failure.

I'm sure you believe you are destined for more. I know you feel like you are worthy of living an inspired life or you wouldn't be reading this book, but up until this point, you may have had a few fantasies about how that is actually achieved. By the time you have finished the book, you will understand how some of those fantasies are ridiculously unrealistic, but more importantly, when you apply what I share, you will learn that reaching a true level of freedom is much easier than you thought.

TOP TIP

Low self-worth is a silent killer of wealth. Self-worth is not necessarily correlated to confidence, popularity, funniness or charisma. It's much deeper than that. Your true level of self-worth is stored in a place that's far more deeply embedded than the masks and the personas you may wear in public.

8
Taking Control Of Your Life

Before money was invented, one person could say to another, 'I've ripped my loin cloth and I know you are handy at making clothing. When you get five minutes, could you make me a new one?'

The other might reply, 'Sure, and when my mother needs open heart surgery because of her clogged artery, I know where to send her because you are by far the best guy for that sort of thing.'

There will always be people who want to work harder and serve more than others, and there comes a point when someone doesn't give fair exchange for a favour done by another. In the example above, saving someone's life hardly equates to stitching up an old piece of clothing, so there needs to be a way of benchmarking the value of the talents people have and how they use those talents to serve others in the world.

That's why money was created. Money is the exchange for levels of services and goods that people are willing to provide or create and deliver to the market. The great thing about money is that it doesn't discriminate. It doesn't care about what colour, race or class you are, and every day starts with a clean slate. The money is already there. It moves around people who are providing value in the form of goods and services. It's no coincidence that the word 'currency' is used for types of money because it's like a current in the water, continuously flowing from person to person. Someone's spending is someone else's income. Someone's income is someone else's spending.

It's the fairest tool ever used.

When Mark Zuckerberg created Facebook and delivered a product to the marketplace that billions of people loved, the world didn't print an extra $100 billion for him.[20] The money was already in existence and circulation. He simply accumulated that $100 billion by providing value that made a vast amount of people and companies on the planet want to give him their money.

---

20 T Mohamed, 'Meet the 16 members of the $100 billion club – who are jointly worth more than Amazon or Google', *Business Insider* (16 September 2024), www.businessinsider.com/wealth-billionaires-musk-bezos-zuckerberg-net-worth-jensen-huang-waltoans-2024-8, accessed 16 October 2024

Is he bad? Is he evil? No. He attracted his money because he wasn't afraid to. He wasn't negatively charged towards money, so he allowed it to flow into his possession.

Quality questions

The good news is, you can shift wealth building up your list of priorities and values quite easily by being conscious of how it will enhance and accentuate your other high values. You can start to do this by asking some questions of yourself.

In Part 2, I explained the effect of taking advice from people who do not have the results you want in life, but it's also important to understand that there are different ways to question your own actions, too. The way you ask questions of yourself can dramatically increase or reduce the opportunities you take advantage of, how you grow and how you spend your time on Earth.

Growing up, I was surrounded by people asking, 'How can I possibly afford to do what I want to do?' whether that was going on holiday, starting a business, buying a new car or just having some time off from work. I noticed that when people received a tax bill or a parking fine, they would ask, 'Why does this have to happen to me?'

I later realised that by structuring questions this way, they were actually turning them into uninspiring ones. When a question is uninspiring, not only does it prevent you from being inspired to find an answer, it also requires greater motivation to look for that answer or solution because you are fixating on an obstruction.

Whatever we focus our attention and energy on, we manifest in our lives. This is the law of attraction. That means if you are focusing on uninspiring questions, then – guess what – you will find uninspiring answers.

Imagine if you rephrase a question from 'Why does this always happen to me?' to 'How can I stop this from happening to me in the future?' Your attention would shift from being a victim to being a master in control of the outcome. You would focus on strategy.

Whatever questions you ask of yourself, you will find the answer to. If you ask questions that require you to look for blame, lack of responsibility, dependency and hard luck, you will find those answers. If you ask questions that force you to look for ownership, mastery, control, accountability and liberation, you will find those answers too.

Here are a few questions you can ask of yourself to start changing your life. I want you to ponder these questions. Give them some real thought and answer them in detail.

1. **If I had one year to live, what would I absolutely love to spend that year doing?** This question brings objectives that are truly meaningful to you into your consciousness. Ask this question regularly.

2. **How can I get paid to do what I love?** I hear many people, particularly in business, say, 'How can I afford to do what I want to do?' They are of the opinion and belief that if they have the money first, they can do everything they want to do.

I have learned to rephrase this question to, 'How can I get paid to do what I want to do?' By structuring the question this way, you allow yourself to be creative and figure out how you can get paid to take the next step. If you love photography and travelling, how could you package a week-long retreat that allows you to charge people who love the same things to learn how to use a camera and have the opportunity to capture some of the most beautiful monuments in an ancient city? If you love Flamenco dancing, how could you get paid to do it? Could you package up a four-day trip to Spain for like-minded individuals where they will learn from a Spanish Flamenco dancer and charge well enough to receive a nice income?

If you are scaling your business, how can you do it for free? How can you exchange services with someone who has what you need? How can you structure a partnership of fair exchange to avoid sacrificing liquidity? How can you get paid to launch your product without it being finished?

3. What are five things I can do today to move closer towards doing what I love? Asking this question every day will allow you to focus on moving towards your most inspired life. The actions do not have to be significant. They can be as small as writing a plan or a list of tasks you would like to delegate.

Working on this daily will inevitably move you closer to your goals.

4. What problems might I face and how can I ensure I have a plan in advance to solve them? Asking this question allows you to build plans, strategies and contingencies so you are not in a reactive state when problems and obstacles inevitably show up.

5. What worked for me this week and what didn't work? Keep a journal so you can efficiently move towards your goals. How could you do things better or more effectively? Ask yourself how your experience (positive or negative) served you and helped you move closer to your inspired life instead of asking how it held you back. There will always be benefits to focus on instead of drawbacks.

6. How will building wealth and achieving financial freedom be of benefit and service to myself and others? Write fifty answers.

7. How will mastering the art of investing be of benefit and service to myself and others? Write fifty answers.

Asking these questions will help you focus on your mission and allow you to control your life instead of life controlling you. Life doesn't just happen to you. You can take it by the horns and navigate it to where you want to go.

You will never please everyone

Trying to please everyone will stop you achieving financial freedom. It will keep you in mediocrity. Everyone has different ideas about what is a good idea.

I receive weekly messages from people telling me that they really want to go after their dreams, but they are afraid of what their mum or dad will say because they wanted them to be a doctor or a lawyer etc, or they tell me that their friends or partners are unsupportive of their ideas and will disapprove. As a result, they back down and give up on going after what they want.

Some people promote peace on Earth; some people promote war and violence. Some people protest against abortions; some people protest in favour of abortions. Some people hunt and kill beautiful animals for no reason; some people are vegan animal activists. Some people cover their entire bodies with a burka; some people show off their naked bodies on social media platforms and glamour magazine publications.

The point is, whatever you say, believe or have an opinion on, there will be a good percentage of the population who have the opposite opinion. This includes your family and friends. Everyone has a different value system.

Understand that as you go after your goals, grow your wealth or scale your business, the more influential you will become and the greater your following will be. If you have six friends and three of them disagree with your goals and turn on you, you might think that's not a big deal, but as your circle of influence grows, the actual size of the percentage that disagrees gets bigger and bigger. If you have an unrealistic fantasy that everyone will like you and your opinions, it will be much harder for you to deal with the growing population who don't.

The common misfortune that happens here is that people end up dimming their light and settling for a small circle of influence while trying to keep everyone happy. The moment you give yourself permission to be authentic and true to your values and focus on your mission with the expectation of losing a few people along the way is the moment you start moving forward and mastering your life.

Living in other people's values will get you nowhere. When you are on death's door, those people will not care what you have or haven't achieved in your life. Only you will. Remember, financial freedom is two words. The freedom part comes from first having a free mind. If you don't have a free mind, you will never achieve freedom of any sort, no matter how much money you earn or how well you manage it.

Money is nothing but a tool of opportunity

As we saw at the start of the chapter, money is neither positive nor negative; it is a medium for fair exchange. Just like words are a vehicle of communication between people, money is a method of communication between value systems.

If you are to attract money and wealth, it's important to have a balanced view on the purpose of money, otherwise you will have difficulty both making it and keeping any money that you do make. Depending on your perceptions towards money, you may even be embarrassed or ashamed of any you have in your possession, which will make it extremely difficult to make any more.

Growing up on a council estate, I heard things like, 'Money doesn't grow on trees', 'Money is evil', 'Money doesn't buy happiness' and so on. These are all negative statements linked to money. When people tell themselves these things and then accumulate money, they often either feel as though they don't deserve it or think it's dirty or evil so they repel it.

When the people on my estate used to fantasise over what they would do if they won the lottery, they would reel off a list of things they would buy and they had spent it all within thirty seconds. They were getting rid of the money entirely before it was even in their possession as though they were not worthy of keeping it.

Another common phrase you hear from people who do not value money is, 'Money isn't important.' Isn't it interesting that people who say money isn't important and don't appreciate it end up working their whole lives for it?

People who understand the value of money, appreciate it and use it as a tool are the ones who become time free.

I would argue that money is one of the most important things in the world. Yes, your family and loved ones are important too, but think about this. To live well and be healthy, you must have at least these things:

- Good food and clean water. Everyone needs food and water to live, no argument.
- Shelter, warmth and security. We need a roof over our heads to protect us and our loved ones from weather and other dangers.

All of these physiological needs cost money. A house costs money, food and water cost money, clothes cost money, toiletries and pharmaceutical products cost money.

We must get our head around the fact that money is important because if we don't have our physiological needs met, our spirit is going to be pretty low. If money isn't as important as family, why the heck do most people spend at least eight hours per day, five days a week sitting in an office or at a place of work that statistics say they hate?[21] Why on Earth do they spend time travelling to and from work, send emails late at night, work overtime or spend time on call at weekends? Why when they are at home are they thinking about work most of the time, even if they would likely say their family is more important than money if you asked them?

The answer, of course, is because they need money. That is nothing to feel guilty about.

The truth is, people who work in a job they hate, spending time away from their family, most likely do so as a result of what they heard about money growing up. Without realising it, people who are going through life with a scathing outlook towards those

---

21 Staff Squared, 'Why 85% of people hate their jobs' (3 December 2019), https://staffsquared.com/blog/why-85-of-people-hate-their-jobs, accessed 17 October 2024

with money are continuing to consider being successful as a negative thing.

Why am I telling you this? I want you to be unstoppable when it comes to becoming financially free. Along the journey, people will come to you with their opinions about money. There will be those who label money good or evil, those who become infatuated by or resentful of it, and those who allow it to run their life instead of them running their money. I want you to be armed with a response so that guilt and shame don't stop you in your tracks.

People who understand and run money value themselves. I want you to be one of these people.

Think back to the money stories exercise you completed in Chapter 2. Look at the beliefs you identified and examine them for any sign of half-truths now that you have learned a little more.

Here are some of the common beliefs people hold about money. Be honest if any strike a chord with you:

- Money is the root of all evil.
- Money is dirty.
- I don't deserve to be rich.
- Money is only made by greedy people.
- Money corrupts.

- You mustn't brag about money and must never say how much you earn, or how much you paid for something unless it was a bargain.
- You will lose friends if you get rich.
- You have to work too hard to be rich.
- There's no such thing as being rich and happy.
- The more you have, the more you will want.
- It's better to be poor.

You probably already understand the opportunity that money can provide, but if you agreed with any of the statements above, work out why. I like to use a simple exercise called The Three Whys to do this. I have used this exercise to build products, solve meaningful problems and negotiate with people in the past.

EXERCISE: The three whys

Ask yourself why you feel the way you do for each statement you agreed with. It might be that you believe money is dirty because one of your parents told you it was, for example.

Once you have the first answer, ask yourself why you gave that answer. Where did it come from? In the example above, it might be that your mum saw her parents arguing about money all the time when she was growing up, and blamed money for their breakup or divorce. She then repeated her belief about money being dirty to you as a child.

The final why goes even further. In the example, you would ask why your mum blamed money for her parents' divorce. It might be that they were arguing because they didn't have enough money to provide the care and attention to their loved ones that they would have liked.

If you dig deeper into a belief in this way, it helps you to see where that belief might have come from. When you can do this rationally, without emotion, you neutralise those negative beliefs. You take away their power and hold over you.

The aim of this exercise is to neutralise all your negative thoughts about money and replace them with a new list of positive beliefs that will allow you to attract as much money as you deserve into your possession.

TOP TIP

The quality of your life depends on the quality of the questions you ask of both yourself and others. Yes, you want to question everything, but ask quality questions too. A quality life deserves quality questions.

9
Your Route To Financial Freedom

What is financial freedom? Some people think financial freedom is achieved by having a lot of money or saving every penny they earn. Some believe it is working their way up in a corporation and growing their income. Some think it is down to a hot stock tip, while for others, financial freedom is being able to travel the world doing what they want.

The truth is that focusing on one particular thing will not get you to financial freedom. The reason people find financial freedom so difficult to achieve is not because it's hard; it's because they simply don't know where they are right now, what strings they must pull to accelerate their journey and what poor actions might hinder them.

I know people who have a low income. They save every penny they earn and have lots of money in the bank, yet they have no life. They are disempowered. I know people who appear to have an amazing lifestyle and yet they have to work eighty hours a week to afford it. I know people who have a mobile and flexible income with no savings. They spend time worrying and panicking about where the next portion of income is coming from.

Most people have a desire to achieve financial freedom, but they usually have no definition of what this actually is to measure their progress. Imagine setting off on a car journey using satellite navigation, and instead of showing the directions, it only showed the destination. You would get lost and probably turn back.

Planning for financial freedom

Financial freedom is a term that is used so flippantly these days, it's no wonder people spend a long time trying to achieve it. Just like any goal, you must have a plan if you want to achieve financial freedom. Most people set goals, but very few *plan* goals.

When I was twenty-two, I knew that if I was to achieve financial freedom, I had to first of all define what it was, and then set milestones and measurable steps to get there. I broke them down into two major phases.

Financial freedom is all about assets.

We will be talking a lot about assets through the rest of this book but an easy to remember objective is:

A – Audit your numbers
S – Simplify your lifestyle
S – Scale leveraged income streams
E – Expand investments
T – Track and Tweak

For the rest of this book, I am going to show you how to do all this.

Phase 1 – Financial independence (The 4 Ps)

My definition of financial independence is being able to generate an income high enough to cover your lifestyle costs regardless of The 4 Ps:

- **Proprietor.** You can generate income without relying on a boss, manager, up-line or peer.

- **Person.** You can generate income without relying on a parent, husband, wife, guardian or partner.

- **Position.** You can generate income without relying on a specific role, down-line or corporate structure.

- **Place.** You can generate income without relying on being in a specific geographical location.

If you are not in this phase, then this is your primary goal. The feeling of freedom comes from being flexible, mobile and nimble. Most of this is achieved in Phase 1.

If you follow and implement what I am going to share with you, financial independence can be achieved in a short space of time. It simply requires a certain focus on three major components. I'll explain these in greater detail shortly, but for now they are:

1. Your liquid assets (LAs)
2. Your lifestyle expenses (LEs)
3. Your leveraged income (LI)

The closer you move towards financial independence, the freer you will feel, but there is a sustainability issue with Phase 1. Although you are able to generate income to cover your lifestyle costs completely independently of a proprietor, person, position or place, which is amazing, it still requires you to be an active part of the process.

Phase 2 – Financial freedom (The 4 Es)

My definition of financial freedom is being able to maintain Phase 1 income regardless of The 4 Es:

- **Economy**. The market can boom and bust without affecting your income.
- **Expertise**. You can lose your mental ability without affecting your income.

- **Energy.** You can lose your physical ability without affecting your income.
- **Existence.** You can cease to exist without affecting your income.

Once you reach Phase 2, you no longer have to do anything for your income. You have achieved complete financial freedom.

Phase 2 is more of a scaling process, depending on how you grow your lifestyle and what type of legacy you want to leave. I achieved Phase 2 within four years, meaning that I could sustain an income for my family without me being here on Earth while maintaining a certain lifestyle. More on this later.

The Freedom Formula – Phase 1

As mentioned, Phase 1 is achieved by focusing on a relationship between three components. Your LAs are how much liquidity you have, including cash, savings, bonds, funds etc. To achieve financial independence, your focus is to increase this figure. Your LEs are how you control your lifestyle costs. The focus here is to reduce, control and scale them proportionally to your liquidity. The type of income you generate will play a part in your prosperity, so your LI is not just time-for-money income. LI is the ability to use assets and skills to generate income that is both mobile and passive.

When people think of passive income, they usually confuse it with mobile income. Passivity is a measurement of time, and mobility is a measurement of space. I could sit on a beach in Bali, Australia, Miami or the Maldives generating income from trading, but it would still require my time. By definition, this would be mobile income and not passive income.

The amount of time it takes you to generate the same amount of income will determine how passive it is. For me, passive income takes me less than one hour per year to generate. Pure passive income is, of course, income that requires none of your time. In the above example, passive income would be someone trading for me while I was sitting on the beach.

There is always a dynamic scale of mobility and passivity. Something that currently takes you eight hours to do can be made more passive if it subsequently takes seven hours to do the same task. If you can do your job from anywhere in the city, you could make it more mobile and do it anywhere in the world, and so on.

Let's explore how the relationship between the three components LAs, LEs and LI plays a part in achieving financial and time freedom.

The time-freedom formula looks like this:

$$LAs \div (LEs - LI) = \text{Time freedom}$$

Example 1: Let's say you have £5,000 in savings (LAs) and your LEs are £2,000 per month. If your only income came from a job or other active income streams and you had no LI streams, your freedom figure would be two months.

$$5{,}000 \div (2{,}000 - 0) = 2.5 \text{ months}$$

You could essentially buy 2.5 months into the future based on your current lifestyle costs if you lost your active income today.

Example 2: In this example, let's say you have the same LAs, the same LEs and you have increased your LI streams to £1,000 per month.

$$5{,}000 \div (2{,}000 - 1{,}000) = 5 \text{ months}$$

You would have now doubled the time you can buy into the future, five months.

Example 3: In this example, everything is the same except you have increased your LI streams by £899 per month. Based on the formula, you now have forty-nine months of freedom. You can buy forty-nine months into the future.

$$5{,}000 \div (2{,}000 - 1{,}899) = 49 \text{ months}$$

As you can see, the freedom figure becomes exponential the closer you meet your LEs with your LI streams.

I have shown examples using fixed LAs and LEs, but the amounts in each of these examples and the relationship between them will determine how much time one can buy into the future. If you have less income, you naturally have fewer LEs, and therefore the easier it is to become financially independent. The financial element simply underpins and supports that lifestyle so you can always choose something different.

Although Phase 1 is a great place to be, there is still an unsustainability issue as you are required to do something. That's where Phase 2 becomes the focus.

The Freedom Formula – Phase 2

If you were able to cover your living costs, what figure would you need invested and managed passively to generate an infinite return on your money without eating into your investment capital?

We are going to go deep into the strategy side of this later, but for now, work out your ideal annual living costs and then divide that figure by 0.08. For example, if your ideal annual living costs total £55,000, then the formula would be:

$$55{,}000 \div 0.08 = £687{,}500$$

This would be the ballpark figure you would need invested, returning an average of 8% per annum, to cover your living costs without any requirement of you.

There are some other variables to consider in this equation which we will cover later, including your returns performance, inflation, other assets, levels of speculation, income growth etc, but I just wanted to share this now to help you get your head around the relationship between liquidity and financial freedom.

A note about debt

There are different kinds of debt. Don't be scared of debt, but be aware of which type affects your freedom and which type doesn't.

You may have heard some debt referred to as good debt and some as bad debt. This can be a deceptive way of looking at the different types of debt because good and bad are subjective. I prefer to categorise debt into cash-flow producing debt and non-cash-flow producing debt. One takes money away, one generates money.

According to the World Bank Group's report on international debt statistics, 76% of the first-world adult population spends as much income as they earn on non-cash-flow producing debt and depreciating consumables.[22] Of those adults, 29% spend more income than they earn on these things. In some countries, such as Australia, the average adult spends over 200%

---

22 World Bank Group, International Debt Statistics, www.worldbank.org/en/programs/debt-statistics/ids, accessed 17 October 2024

of their income on non-cash-flow producing debt.[23] People in the Netherlands and Denmark spend closer to 300%.[24]

That means the average Dutch and Danish adult is spending three times their income on debts. Think about that for a minute.

Here's the important point. The amount of money you spend on non-cash-flow producing debt is directly correlated to your emotional wellbeing and feeling of prosperity. The reason people take on non-cash-flow producing debt is usually to keep up with others or to pay for a treat to escape reality for a moment and reward themselves for putting up with their life. The amount of this kind of debt you take on will affect how you speak to clients and your family. It will affect your mood, your health and your quality of life.

A cash-flow producing debt is one that generates income to contribute to the monthly payments of the debt. Why is this important? Taking on cash-flow producing debt can be good for building wealth, but the thing to realise here is the impact each type of debt will have on you and how it will affect your probability of achieving financial freedom.

---

23 W Jolly, Australian Household Debt Statistics 2024 (Jacaranda Finance, 29 August 2024), www.jacarandafinance.com.au/general/average-household-debt-statistics, accessed 17 October 2024

24 M Comelli, 'Why northern Europe is so indebted' (The Loop, 26 February 2021), https://theloop.ecpr.eu/why-northern-europe-is-so-indebted, accessed 17 October 2024

Percentage of debt vs income chart

During 2020 and the economically crippling Covid pandemic, I was inundated with messages from people telling me that the lockdown was the best thing that could have happened to them. Because they couldn't go out, they had learned to appreciate what they had and realised just how little they needed to be happy. At the same time, they had a real taste of financial freedom: passive income in the form of government cheques. They could get up each day and decide what they would love to work on first. They also cleared more unnecessary expenses and debts than ever, which allowed them to free up their mind and enhance their mood.

There will be certain debts that make you feel stressed and certain debts that do not. This is all down to the ratio between your total income and the total debt repayment figure. The amount of debt you have relative to your income will determine how you feel and cash-flow producing debt can help. However, you need to understand the relationship of the ratio and how to calculate it.

If you add up your total debt repayments and then divide them by your total income, you will get a figure which can be multiplied by 100 for a percentage. This is called a debt to income (DTI) ratio. If your debt repayments are £1,500 per month and your income is £2,500 per month, your DTI will look like this:

$$1{,}500 \div 2{,}500 \times 100 = 60\%$$

This means that 60% of your income is going towards debt. Your percentage score will be directly correlated to how you feel and the quality of your life.

<10%: Excellent. You feel free and nimble. You have the flexibility to be proactive and not reactive when it comes to your financial decisions. You are controlling your finances instead of your finances controlling you.

10%–20%: Very good. You still have everything under control, but as you approach 20%, you are just at the limit before feeling a pinch.

20%–30%: Leveraged. You are now feeling like you took on a little too much debt and probably that you need to work an extra shift to make up for it, which has put a bit of pressure on you.

30%–50%: Stretched. You feel maxed out and probably work every hour to ensure you make the payments. You have spent money before you earned the right to and you may start to resent the purchases that you took on the debt for.

50%–75%: Stressed. You are losing sleep. You worry every day about how much you owe and you start to lose sight of the light at the end of the tunnel. You are showing up as a pretender spender and as a result, you are on a treadmill of unhappiness.

75%–100%: Working for the bank. At this point you are just existing. You are working every hour for the bank. You owe the lending institutions every penny you earn and you feel completely disempowered.

>100%: Enslaved. You pray for a lottery win or an inheritance. Your brain has gone so far into survival mode that you cannot even think of a feasible way out. Bankruptcy or jail seem like your only options.

The reason this calculation is so powerful is because it takes into consideration cash-flow producing debt and allows you to take on that kind of debt without affecting your score. This way you can scale your lifestyle and use cash-flow producing debt to your advantage.

For example, if you took on a cash-flow producing debt and the monthly repayments were £1,000, while the debt itself produced £1,000 in income each month, then it would cancel itself out. The formula would allow you to take on that debt without it affecting your financial and mental wellbeing.

If you keep your DTI below 20% at all times, you will find that you are more creative, more focused, more proactive and more likely to build wealth.

Lastly, paying down a debt is a guaranteed return on investment (ROI). If you invested your money into the stock market and yielded a 10% return, you would pay tax on that, which would net you 7%, say. Paying off high-interest debt gives you a guaranteed return on your money. For example, if you invest in the stock market and earn a 10% return, you might only keep around 7% after taxes. But if you pay off a debt with a 10% APR, you're effectively getting a 10% return, tax-free, because you're no longer losing that money to interest. So, if your debt interest rate is higher than what you'd expect to earn from investing, it often makes more financial sense to pay off the debt first.

To work out what the equivalent investment would be to paying down debt, use this formula:

$$\text{Equivalent investment} = \text{Debt APR} / (1 - \text{your tax rate}).$$

I hope that's given you an insight into types of debt and their potential impact. I'll be covering debt again later, including strategies and goals.

TOP TIP

The common misconception is that the feeling of freedom is created solely by finances. In fact, the feeling of freedom is mostly made up of being mobile, flexible and choosing how you organise your day. Many people became a lot freer during the Covid pandemic when everyone was forced towards remote working and felt liberated by this process.

10
Mobility Freedom – Designing Your Inspired Life

Now that we've explored mindset and identity, it's time to talk about the second essential freedom: Mobility Freedom. This is your ability to live, work and experience life on your own terms. Where you want, when you want and with whom you want.

There are certain things we must do, there are certain things we feel we should do, there are certain things we love to do and there are certain things that we do for fair exchange, reward or remuneration. My definition of living an inspired life is being able to wake up and spend the majority of each and every day prioritising tasks that we love and choose to do while being paid for doing them. When our daily actions align with our highest values and we are able to delegate any uninspiring tasks, we are living true to ourselves.

If you spend every day doing what you love doing, but you aren't being paid for it, you will become resentful. If you are being highly paid, but you hate what you are doing, you will feel unrewarded. If you are doing what you love and being highly paid, but not providing value to anyone, you will feel unfulfilled.

Every human being wants to feel fulfilled, be rewarded and spend their time doing what they love doing. The key is to have all three.

I find the tasks that are both uninspiring to me and difficult to delegate are those I resent the most. The tasks I love doing that provide me with reward and fulfilment are the most inspiring.

An inspired life is being free enough to focus on our most meaningful work without turmoil. When we are free to focus on work that is meaningful to us, and we are able to pay for our lifestyle doing so, we become more caring, more loving, more supportive, more creative and more inspired. In this state, we become better human beings.

To have mobility freedom, there are four important indicators that can be measured and improved, and a four-step protocol to improve your life:

> **M** – Mandatory tasks: I can delegate, automate or remove many of my daily obligations
> **O** – Operational flexibility: I can work productively from anywhere
> **V** – Value alignment: I spend most of my time on tasks that inspire me
> **E** – Experiential freedom: I can travel, explore or pause my routine at will

To improve mobility freedom, use the FLOW Framework:

> **F** – Filter your task list
> **L** – Leverage your income
> **O** – Optimise location independence
> **W** – Work from inspiration

I will start introducing some of this protocol here, and continue in Chapter 14.

This is your life. Fill it with inspiration.

Delegation

If you want to become *Always Free*, you must master the art of delegation.

EXERCISE: Time study

The best way to gauge where you are at right now is to carry out a time study.

There are 168 hours in a week. For an entire week, commit to setting an alarm every 30 minutes (apart from when you are asleep) and write down exactly what you have been doing for the last half hour. Use categories for tasks such as eating, admin, emails, washing, gym etc. Don't act differently or make different decisions just because you are doing the experiment. At the end of the week, you will see a heat map of exactly how you spend your time.

Once you have completed the initial part of the test, the next thing to do is to add up all the time you spent in each category. This will give you a clear indication of what you spend most of your time doing (do not include sleep).

Order the categories from highest time spent to lowest time spent, then give each task a score from 0–10 based on how inspired you felt to do that particular task, 10 being tasks that you love and choose to do, 0 being tasks you must do, but hate.

Now that you have identified the low-inspirational tasks, the plan is to prioritise delegating those from your responsibility.

What you will find is the low-inspirational tasks you undertake are those that you cannot either monetise or delegate easily. The high-inspirational tasks that you undertake are those that you love to do, can monetise and can delegate if you want to.

Ask yourself how you can delegate the low-inspirational tasks. Prioritise the delegation process.

You may decide to get rid of some tasks altogether. If scrolling on social media is not inspiring and you don't love doing it, then just stopping it can buy you back that time to work on more inspiring tasks. Seek to implement these changes in order of inspiration, dumping and delegating everything that doesn't inspire you, while focusing on monetising only that which you choose to or love to do.

Beware of 'delegator's block'. This is an emotional phenomenon that keeps us enslaved to uninspiring tasks through the fear that no one else can do as good a job as we can. Systemise your task, build in quality control measures, find the right person, train them up, release your need for control… and you'll thank yourself for it in the long run.

Your focus for guaranteed financial freedom

To become wealthy and financially free, focusing on one system is extremely risky and will have a low success rate. I prefer to promote a guaranteed strategy for becoming financially free.

There are six areas of focus that, if mastered, will guarantee your financial freedom and ability to live an inspired life. If even one of these areas is neglected, you will limit your chances of building a sustainable, free and inspired life, and restrict your potential for maximum fulfilment.

Objective

It's important to know what you want in life and even more important to know why you want it. Clarity over your purpose, focusing on your inspired mission and having a cause beyond yourself is a fundamental stepping stone to building an extraordinary life of fulfilment and reward.

Time is your most valuable asset. When you have a cause beyond yourself, you no longer get distracted with day-to-day turmoil.

Mindset

There is no doubt that you need a strong mindset to achieve an extraordinary life. Giving yourself permission to put yourself first and go after your dreams is a true superpower.

The degree to which you can see everything as being 'on the way' instead of 'in the way' will dictate how efficiently you evolve and move towards mastery.

Income

Earning more money can be extremely advantageous when you're building wealth, but depending on the type of income and the lack of diversity in earning it, it can also become extremely stressful if not managed wisely. Trading time for money takes the focus off the mission and significantly limits your potential to build sustainable and long-lasting wealth that you can enjoy.

Understanding how to shift from active income to mobile and passive income streams will liberate you. You will be more vibrant, have more energy and life force. As a result, you will naturally earn more money.

Lastly, knowing to allocate that income to paying your true self first is what will set you aside from the majority of the population.

Lifestyle

Everyone can and should have nice things, but there is a fine line between prosperity and accidentally becoming enslaved to the wage because of poor planning or no structure around the priorities and ratios of lifestyle growth. Balancing these can help you empower your senses and get the experiences you want in life for yourself and your loved ones. The trappings of 'assumed' wealth can be deadly.

It's normally those who have a strong focus on their own values and mission that dictate to others how they should spend their money. When you stop subordinating to other people's values when they are telling you how to spend your money, you can take control of your own scalability and have whatever you want while still building wealth.

Liquidity

Having a focus on liquidity is essential. You need cash to pay for your lifestyle. The ability to be nimble and flexible allows you the breathing room you need to be more free.

When you focus on time being the objective, you must shift your attention to liquidity and the importance of building as much as you can. Then you remain nimble and flexible to dance with the rhythms of life on your terms.

Investing and speculation

People who learn the secrets of investing that have stood the test of time will prosper. It's one of the most powerful wealth acceleration vehicles on the planet; use it to your advantage sustainably and consistently.

Being able to have your money work for you will allow you to rapidly grow wealth. The stock markets have risen in value year-on-year by 10% on average since they began.[25] When you invest in the best-performing markets in the world, you can seriously accelerate your run to financial freedom. Access to leverage and speculation can be exploited through skill and is one of the most liberating income streams known to humankind.

Time to set a benchmark

If you want to achieve success at anything, you must first have a tangible way to measure your current situation so that you can set a benchmark for improvement.

I am going to ask you ten questions that will allow you to put a stake in the ground and raise your consciousness and awareness on your financial independence journey. These questions are designed to identify any naiveties towards building wealth and highlight the importance of liquidity. You can come back to these again once you have completed the book, when you will understand them even better, but it's important you consider your answers at this stage to bring out your consciousness and awareness of where you are right now in your wealth journey.

I encourage you to write these questions out and answer them as well as you can before continuing.

---

25 T Campbell, J Safane, 'Average stock market return: A historical perspective and future outlook' *Business Insider* (25 September 2024), www.businessinsider.com/personal-finance/investing/average-stock-market-return#, accessed 18 October 2024

Ten questions

Question 1. Do you want financial freedom?

The answer to this question may seem obvious initially, but many people seem to think that they want something because they look up to others who have it. When they really think about the result and the work required to get the result, they realise it isn't what they want at all. If they really wanted it, they would be going after it and likely already have some results. They may have even achieved it.

You may feel like you want financial freedom, but the truth is, until now, it simply hasn't been high enough a priority in your values for you to go and achieve it. You are now seeking guidance from someone who has already invested their time, money and resources into researching and actually implementing it, which is great, but if you are not that inspired to achieve financial freedom, it would be wise to write down what is highest on your values list right now. Then write a list of 50 to 100 reasons why achieving financial freedom will help you enhance, exaggerate and fulfil your highest values.

Question 2. What is the total value of all of your LAs right now?

LAs include assets such as cash, savings, short-term investments, funds, electronic funds transfers (ETFs), bonds, individual savings accounts (ISAs) etc. Ideally, an LA is any asset whereby you can withdraw cash within a two- to three-day time frame.

I don't like to advise you to add house equity into this answer because it's reliant upon a housing market value, which fluctuates with demand. You then need to go through the process of selling the house to access the cash. A house is a non-liquid asset because you cannot access the cash within a two- to three-day time frame.

That being said, if you have equity in a home, I would encourage you to complete these ten questions using both examples, ie including your home equity and not including your home equity. This will really open your eyes to the difference liquidity can make to your financial freedom journey and get you thinking in terms of liquidity, flexibility and freedom.

Finally, you may want to consider adding in some items of jewellery if you own sought-after pieces that you have a degree of certainty would sell quickly should you put them up for auction or sale.

Question 3. What are you total liabilities?

Calculate the total of all finance, loans, IOUs etc that comprise your debt. This should include all monies owed to lenders, including interest. Again, you can do this exercise including your mortgage if you have one, and then without including the mortgage to see the difference.

Question 4. What is your net worth?

This will be the answer you gave to Question 2 minus the answer you gave in Question 3.

If you deduct all of your liabilities from your LAs, you get your net worth. If you have been doing the exercise including your home equity, you will see the difference between net worth and financial freedom here. You might have a million sitting as equity in your house and, by definition, be a millionaire on paper, but you won't have the freedom you seek because you would have to sell the house to realise that million to pay for your lifestyle.

Question 5. What exactly is the annual income that you would need to generate passively to cover your ideal LEs?

In other words, what is the total annual income that you would need to survive and maintain your ideal lifestyle? Calculate this over a twelve-month period and write down the answer. Include all your outgoings over the year plus any additional expenses you would need to cover to have your ideal lifestyle.

An easy way to reach a realistic figure here is to go over your bank statements from the last twelve months and add up the total, then divide it by twelve to get a monthly average. This way you will include all of the one-offs such as car maintenance, holidays, vet bills etc.

Once you have the answer to this question, you will have a tangible figure to aim for to reach financial independence, and ultimately financial freedom.

Question 6. What percentage ROI or interest rate are you confident you can currently yield over a twelve-month period on average?

If you currently have rental properties generating 4% ROI on average per year, you would write down 4%. If you are a speculative trader or an investor, you might be generating 10%, 20% or more ROI. Write down the percentage figure that you are confident you can generate year-on-year as an average or mean.

The key here is to lower your expectations. If you have been investing for the last two years and you managed to generate 20% last year, but only 3% the year before, then your average would be 11.5% over the period.

If you have savings in a bank, you might only be generating 1% interest per year. In that case, check what the average interest rate has been for the last twenty years and write that percentage down.

Remember, the stock market has gone up 10% on average year-on-year for almost 100 years.[26] If you are unsure as to the answer to this question, I suggest you write down 6%, which would be the absolute minimum conservative return you can achieve if you follow the most basic passive investment strategies laid out in this book.

Question 7. What is the inflation rate on average over the last twenty years in your country?

Again, with this question, you don't want to be thinking year-on-year because it fluctuates. What is the average? Once you know the inflation rate, you can build that into the formula so that as your LEs increase, you can compensate for that to keep your expectations realistic.

Question 8. How much total invested liquidity would you need, taking into consideration the ROI yield from Question 6 and the inflation rate from Question 7, to generate your ideal passive income from Question 5?

As an example here, let's say that you included your equity in your home and that currently stands at £500,000. If you sold your house and liquidated the equity, and then put that money into investments at

---

26 T Campbell, J Safane, 'Average stock market return: A historical perspective and future outlook' *Business Insider* (25 September 2024), www.businessinsider.com/personal-finance/investing/average-stock-market-return#, accessed 18 October 2024

6% per year, that would yield a £30,000 per year passive income for you. Because you have calculated the average return, that means you could generate this level of income without ever depreciating the original investment capital, so if the number you wrote down as your ideal annual LEs was under £30,000, you no longer have to work at that point. You are financially free.

However, that doesn't allow for inflation in your country, which is why you are going to have to take that into account. In this example, you would deduct the average inflation rate from the £30,000, but if you do the maths and the figure is still above your annual LEs, then you have reached financial freedom.

Many times, people get to this point and realise they already have enough equity in their house to be financially free, but because they have never thought about the relationship between liquidity and freedom, it has never crossed their minds to do the maths.

Question 9. What is the shortfall of passive income between the answers to Question 4 and Question 8?

If you do not currently have enough liquidity to invest to cover your ideal LEs as well as inflation, write down how much more you would need to generate the additional monthly passive income stream to make up the difference.

Once you write this number down, you have got something tangible to work on. Not only will you have a tangible figure, you will know the shortfall, which means you will know what you need to generate.

Remember, these questions are designed to calculate what you need to do to achieve complete financial freedom. You will achieve Phase 2 – Financial Freedom in a relatively short space of time using LI streams and the assets you will learn to invest in throughout the rest of this book.

The answer to this question will give you two pieces of valuable information:

- What you need to generate to make up financial freedom
- Where you need to shift your focus

After completing the questions this far, you may already be thinking that you can make up the rest of the passive income through your business, if you have one, via systems, delegations and automations.

Question 10. What is your strategy to achieve financial freedom?

Until now, you may not have had a strategy. By following the strategies in this book, you will no longer view financial freedom as a fluffy goal. You will have a clear direction and the confidence to go and achieve it in the most efficient way possible.

Always Free will shift your mind to think in terms of developing your strategies towards passive and semi-passive incomes and LI streams, making your business, if you have one, and your income more efficient to free up your time rather than you working harder and harder trying to earn more money.

True wealth is not about earning more money. It's about having more free time by managing what you earn. You then inevitably earn more money as a by-product of doing what you love.

Ten answers

Write down your answers and remember, at this stage, it doesn't matter if you cannot answer all the questions yet. This exercise is to open your eyes and highlight vulnerability, naivety and lack of strategy. It will be inspiring for you to revisit these questions twelve months after reading this book and see how different your life looks.

Here are some example answers to the ten questions:

1. Yes!
2. House = £600,000, Rolex = £10,000, cash = £20,000 savings

3. Mortgage = £250,000, loan £5,000
4. £630,000 − £255,000 = £375,000 net worth
5. £2,500 per month = £30,000 per year
6. 8% invested in a Standard & Poor's (S&P) growth fund plus a couple of real estate investment trusts (REITs) and an ISA
7. 2.48%
8. £30,000 ÷ 0.08 = £375,000 + 2.48% = £384,300
9. £384,300 − £375,000 = £9,300 shortfall in LAs
10. Strategy example: Generate a new £200 digitally delivered product online and sell to fifty people. Learn to better my investment returns, learn how to invest, learn to buy high-quality stocks, start accelerating my savings, learn how to efficiently grow my liquidity, focus on isolated education etc.

In this strategy example, you need to come up with an extra £9,300 to never have to work again, if you decide not to. See what I mean when I say, 'Being wealthy isn't about earning more money'?

It's about having time.

The path to financial freedom

Before moving on, I want you to put this book down for a moment and question everything you have read so far.

Question me. Question my values and motives. Question my advice. Question why I wrote this book. Question my results.

Let it all sink in and ask yourself, 'Do I believe that this guy can give me the answers and strategies I need?' Take some time to stalk me on social media and read some reviews to learn what other people are saying about me.

I want you to be 100% certain that you resonate with me and my messages so far before you spend your valuable time reading the rest of this book. Your time is valuable.

I also want you to know that if you are willing to apply what I am about to share, your life will transform forever.

Always Free is now going to focus on clear instructions to become financially free by giving you strategies. To set a benchmark at this point, it would be wise to see how you score currently by taking the freedom profile test at www.alwaysfree.com/freedomtest.

TOP TIP

I am confident that what I have written will enable you to become financially free. The reason I am able to say this with such certainty is because I am living proof. Congruency is an alignment in our thoughts, words and actions. For me, congruency is extremely important. I like to know not only that the person I take advice from has achieved what it is I am striving for, but also that their instructions are not masked with showmanship and fluffy false promises.

PART 4
THE TIERS OF FINANCIAL FREEDOM WEALTH METHOD©

The third freedom, Financial Freedom is about building or acquiring systems and assets that generate income without requiring your constant presence. This chapter will show you how to unlock it.

Money can buy you time. Wealth is how much time you can buy. Link the two and you will have a great life.

My Tiers of Freedom WEALTH method is a process that enabled me to achieve financial freedom. WEALTH comprises:

- **What and why?** How to get closer to your purpose and plan a life that is meaningful and inspiring to you. A life that will drive you to achieve financial freedom.

- **Expenses and expectations.** How to control, optimise and automate your personal finances and build a wealth liquidity system that is primed for maximum acceleration.

- **Asset accumulation.** How to make your money work for you in the most efficient and effective manner using principles that have stood the tests of time.

- **Leverage.** How to use leverage to your advantage. Scale your income to dump as much liquidity into your system as possible while you remain free and nimble to enjoy the lifestyle you want.

- **Trading.** How trading and speculation can be used to assist with the acceleration of your wealth and significantly enhance your returns.

- **Hedging.** How to wisely manage your entire net worth and optimise it for maximum growth and sustainability to stand the test of time.

The chapters in Part 4 of *Always Free* will take a deep dive into each element of WEALTH.

11
What And Why?

Simply having a strategy and a desire to have a nice lifestyle is not enough to help you live an extraordinary life. You need a cause beyond yourself.

There is an abundance of solid strategies for losing weight, starting a business and building wealth. Most people are unsuccessful with these strategies because their motivation and drive are not great enough. People who have a compelling reason to achieve something have a greater chance of getting to where they want to be than people who just have a strategy alone. The motivation is far more important than the strategy because you are likely to have the strategy anyway.

After studying various proprietary trading firms in Wall Street, I discovered that there is a shelf-life for the best-performing traders. They normally start when they are young, driven by money and lifestyle alone. They do well, but after four to five years, they realise that they want to work towards a greater cause. They often leave the prop firm in their mid-twenties to take a path that inspires them.

People who chase lifestyle alone tend to end up plateauing due to feeling unfulfilled, unless they move on to a bigger cause. Knowing what you want is one thing, but having a compelling why will motivate you from within to go and achieve it.

The importance of specific goals

It's common for people to set general goals in life such as losing weight. They might have a brilliant strategy to lose weight, but without specifying a particular amount of weight they would like to lose and a reason they want to lose it, they are unlikely to succeed. The same goes for building wealth and living an inspired life.

We have a built-in inertia when it comes to accumulating money. For every penny we make, our drive for earning more goes down. If you had zero money to your name and I gave you £1, that £1 would make up 100% of your net worth. If you had £10, and I offered you £1, the £1 would make up 10% of your net worth. If you had £1,000 and I offered you £1, that £1 would make up 0.001% of your net worth, and you would value it less than you did when it was equivalent to your entire net worth. This means that as you make more and more money, your drive to make it decreases as you devalue it – unless you have a bigger reason to make more.

In the analogy of weight loss, you find that often the closer people get to their ideal weight, the more they take their foot off the pedal and become lax with their eating habits. They might even reach their ideal weight, then celebrate by eating a large fatty takeaway. As they do not have a cause beyond achieving their ideal weight, they struggle to maintain it and are forever 'battling' with their weight.

In 2016, I ran 10 km each and every day for thirty days for a local children's hospice called Chestnut Treehouse. It was difficult and every day started with me trying to talk myself out of running. Then I thought about the kids I was raising money for and the amazing staff at the hospice. Suddenly, the run became a small problem for me. I had a compelling why that got me through.

You must overshoot your goals instead of just reaching them. In other words, if you want the highest chance of successfully achieving the life you desire, you must have a cause beyond yourself.

Finding your why

Understand that you will never reach a point in your life and say, 'I have made it. I don't want anything else now.' This means that the bigger your cause, the further you can see and plan into the future, the better chance you have of achieving the life you want. Having something huge to pull yourself towards will allow you to be focused and not discouraged by the day-to-day challenges that life throws at you.

When the why is big enough, the hows take care of themselves.

Purpose and inspiration

Let's get clearer about your why. This requires deep thought and self-reflection that is quite difficult to endure, but it is essential.

I have worked with clients who, at fifty-five years old, have only just realised why they are on Earth and what they are here to do. As a result, they have been brought to tears of inspiration. They then go on to create a life they truly want.

Your purpose is the most important and inspiring service and contribution you feel you can make to humanity and/or the world, as well as bringing the most inspiring rewards for yourself. Deep inside your mind, heart and soul there exists an inner yearning; a longing to fully express your most meaningful purpose or primary reason why you feel you exist at this time. This is what I want to help you find.

Living out your purpose is what fulfils any voids.

What do you get up for?

What would you love to do every day even if you didn't get paid?

I have had endless conversations with people who have always been on the search for happiness. They take a course, they learn a skill, they get a job, and the next thing you know, they are taking a different course, learning another skill and getting a new job.

When I talk to these people, they tell me that they are fed up, frustrated or unhappy and they seem to think that if they keep searching, they will find happiness. What they often haven't taken the time to do is get clear on what they actually enjoy. Instead of sitting down and thinking about what lights them up, they keep chasing, chasing, chasing, becoming even more frustrated because they have wasted money and, more importantly, time figuring out what they don't like.

One of the most fundamental human needs is certainty. We like to know that we will be safe. Conversely, another fundamental need is uncertainty. The need to explore. The desire to experience new things. The ambition to test the unknown, grow and improve.

As a result, once people become comfortable and content, they often go on a search for something new. This is because they have satisfied their level of certainty for so long, they now want uncertainty. The problem is, when people search for uncertainty, they often search for something for the sake of it or because they think it will be cool instead of taking actions that are aligned with their true inner values.

When you align your search for uncertainty with your true inner values, you will remain inspired to grow while being motivated to do so, and feel fulfilled at the same time. This provides a new layer of certainty and the cycle spirals upwards.

Making decisions and taking actions aligned with your own instead of other people's values and having your own why will make moving forward to financial independence much easier and far more efficient. To start to understand your purpose, you can do this simple exercise.

EXERCISE: Understanding your purpose

Write down three answers to each of these questions, grading them from the most pertinent to the third-most.

- What do you talk about most? Why?
- What do you spend most of your money on? Why?
- What do you need no motivation to do? Why?
- What are you most disciplined and reliable in? Why?

- What do you spend most of your time doing? Why?
- What do you have most of in your personal space? Why?
- What would be the first three things you would choose to do if money was no object? Why?
- If you only had forty-eight hours to live, what are the top three things you would you spend your time doing? Why?

When you answer all of these questions honestly, you will start to see patterns emerge. Do you notice that any of these common patterns have been caused by voids and a perception of lack in your childhood? Are there any coincidences highlighting why you do what you do now that match experiences in your youth?

Looking at these answers, write a paragraph stating what you would love to be, what you would love to have, and what you would love to be doing five years from now.

Let me know what you wrote by sending me an email at info@graystone.education

---

Once you have your compelling why, your true purpose aligned with your values, it's time to move on and build your wealth liquidity system.

TOP TIP

To achieve financial success, you must accept that you already have the ability to do so. Although there are some external factors you must control and manipulate, it's up to you to find happiness within, and then reverse engineer the process to live an inspired life on your own terms.

12
Expenses And Expectations

Your money should never control you. You are the puppet master. If you are burying your head in the sand, unaware of your spending habits, you will be run by your money.

There have been multiple times in history when the wealth inequality in certain countries has been so vast, governments have carried out wealth redistribution. The purpose of the exercise is to take from the rich via taxes and donations, and give to the poor. Each time this happens, the majority of the wealth ends up back in the hands of the 10% within seven to twelve months.[27]

---

27   M Goldstein, *The Snow Lion And The Dragon: China, Tibet, and the Dalai Lama* (University of California Press, 1997) and B Hillman, 'China's many Tibets: Diqing as a model for "development with Tibetan characteristics?"', Asian Ethinicity (June 2010), www.tandfonline.com/doi/abs/10.1080/14631361003779604, accessed 16 April 2025

This goes to show that money flows from the hands of those who value it least to those who value it most.

You might not currently value money as much as you thought. You might value spending it or giving it away, but not building wealth.

Having answered the ten questions in Chapter 10, you might be thinking about how to put a plan together to get to where you want to be. It starts with understanding your behaviour and habits right now so that you can change them to allow you to build wealth.

When the majority of people get paid, their income gets poured into one metaphorical bucket (their only bank account), and by the end of the month, the bucket is dry. Most of the time, it's not the big living expenses that deplete the bucket, but the hundreds of tiny little ones, the cracks in the bucket that go unnoticed. Death by a thousand paper cuts.

Before you try to build wealth or do anything else, you must first identify the leaks in your bucket.

Stop the bleeding

One of my good friends used to be in the Marines. He was medically trained and was taught that the most important thing to do when he found a casualty in the field who was clearly losing blood was to stop the bleeding before attempting to move them to a safe shelter.

Similarly, imagine if you came home one day to find your house flooding due to a cracked water pipe. While the water was rising, would you stand around scratching your head? Would you look for the number of the insurance company to start a claim process? Would you move your furniture out to the garden to dry it out? Of course not!

The logical first thing to do would be to find the origin of the issue and stop the leak, shutting off the stopcock immediately. Then you can go through the motions of rescuing your possessions and sorting out insurance claims.

If you are to efficiently achieve financial independence, you must understand that with personal finance, trading and investing, cash is the lifeblood. Your cash and liquidity are the lifeline of your freedom, the blood of your financial independence, and because of this, your main priority should be not to lose money unnecessarily.

Plug the leaks

If your income drains through a leak in your metaphorical bucket, the first thing to do is to identify these leaks and patch them up.

Without you realising it, the small transactions, the few pounds each time you swipe your contactless card, can add up and have a huge impact on your journey to financial independence. You're not alone. Many people don't realise what effect this has on their wealth and freedom.

Understand that what gets measured gets improved. Also understand that it's easier and cheaper to save money than to earn more, so you can accumulate more wealth by reducing your expenses than you can by earning the same amount in additional generated income.

Let me give you an example. We have person A and person B, both currently earning the same money and paying out the same expenses.

EXPENSES AND EXPECTATIONS

	Person A	Person B
Income	£2,000	£2,000
Expenses	£1,800	£1,800
Disposable	£200	£200

Person A thinks that if they want to double their disposable income, they must double their earned income. They know that they will raise their living expenses with their income (this is the reason they want more income in the first place), which will keep their margin relatively spaced.

Person A works extremely hard to double their income, and while doing so, doubles their expenses relatively. They end up with an additional £200 disposable income, which means they now have £400 left each month. To do this, they have had to increase their income by 100%.

	Person A	Person B
Income	£4,000	£2,000
Expenses	£3,600	£1,800
Disposable	£400	£200

Person B is much smarter. They decide to go through their expenses with a goal to increase their disposable income. Person B doesn't have to double their actual income to get the same result. Instead, they rationalise and negotiate savings on their outgoings of just 11.11% to get the same result as person A.

1,800 − 11.11% = 1,600 (200 saving)

	Person A	Person B
Income	£4,000	£2,000
Expenses	£3,600	£1,600
Disposable	£400	£400

Do you think you can save 11.11% on your outgoings right now? I am confident you can and I am going to show you not only how to make those savings, but how to optimise them and turn them into actual income.

The first step is to observe your current spending habits.

EXERCISE: Recognising your habits and hot spots

This exercise comes in two parts. If you complete the two parts, you will have a complete mind shift towards how you spend your money.

Part 1:

For the next thirty days, track your spending habits. Doing this will allow you to produce a clear report on your behavioural spending patterns.

Every time you go to buy something, take a note to say what you bought, which category it falls into, ie confectionery, luxury, alcohol, food etc, and log it without changing your behavioural habits. In other words, don't neglect to buy something you would usually buy just because you are conscious of this exercise. It will ruin the results.

There are some great apps online to assist with this exercise that link to your bank and automatically categorise your transactions. Just search for finances tracking applications online.

Part 2:

Once you have completed Part 1, log on to your online banking and go through the last twelve months' bank statements, listing the spending patterns in the same way. I recommend you record this information in separate columns:

- Column 1 – Item of expense (rent, insurance, confectionery etc).
- Column 2 – Category (food, clothes, holiday, utilities etc).
- Column 3 – The current monthly expense in monetary value.
- Column 4 – Was this expense more than you thought? Yes/No.
- Column 5 – Is this expense a debt? Yes/No.

The purpose of Column 4 is to highlight any hot spots. When you add up the amounts over time, they can often be much higher than you expected, and visibly highlighting these hot spots at this stage will not only tighten your awareness of how much you are spending on them, but also help later when you prioritise and optimise the potential saving.

The purpose of Column 5 is to give you an understanding of just how much debt you have and, more importantly, your DTI ratio.

> The biggest step of all here is to get close to your money. Stare your finances in the face and learn to be comfortable doing so. If you can't manage emotions around your own money, you won't be able to manage investments, business, speculation or any other income-generating asset.

Analysing your historic spending habits is the starting point. It will open your eyes and give you a heightened awareness of what your habits are, and raise your consciousness on the importance of keeping track of the little expenses. Get used to staring at your bank balance on a daily basis.

Prioritising your savings

You have been demonstrating your value on financial freedom by looking at the spending patterns from your bank account. Once you understand this, you can start to patch up your leaking bucket.

If you completed the exercise properly, you are probably already excited to make some savings on the hot spots. You may also have made some shocking discoveries in terms of how much money you are wasting each month. That is normal. We are going to change that now.

The next step is to prioritise savings and negotiations. This is a simple process of taking the list of expenses from the last exercise and putting each one through a series of questions. This will allow you not only to prioritise the order in which you start patching up your leaks, but also to organise those leaks in order of complexity and biggest savings.

From the list of expenses, first write down which items you know you can definitely make savings on that are applicable to this exercise. For example, if you can make savings on your mortgage, that would be applicable even though you might not be able to do so until your fixed mortgage rate ends and you renegotiate an offer. The same can be said for insurance premiums and utility bills. They would still be applicable for potential savings, albeit maybe in the future.

There might be some expenses that are not applicable to this part of the process, such as council tax or TV licensing. You may decide to get rid of your TV altogether, but unless you plan on doing that, you cannot negotiate the cost of the licence, so there would be no savings to be made.

Once you have the list, write next to each item your priority of making a saving on it, grading it from 1–10. A good place to start would be to write down all of the hot spots first. The large eye-opening costs you discovered during the previous exercise are usually the low-hanging fruits.

Whenever I go through a process of prioritising savings, I run each expense through a couple of matrices. The first matrix is for critical and highly valued expenses. The purpose of this matrix is to identify which expenses are critical and which expenses are highly valuable to you, but less critical. The great thing about this process is that it allows you to negotiate over the things that inspire you and you really love, so that you don't end up disempowered. In other words, it allows you to get a balance and consider which valuable expenses you want to keep.

Take a look at the illustration of the matrix below and consider organising your saving priorities based on what's critical and what's truly valuable to you.

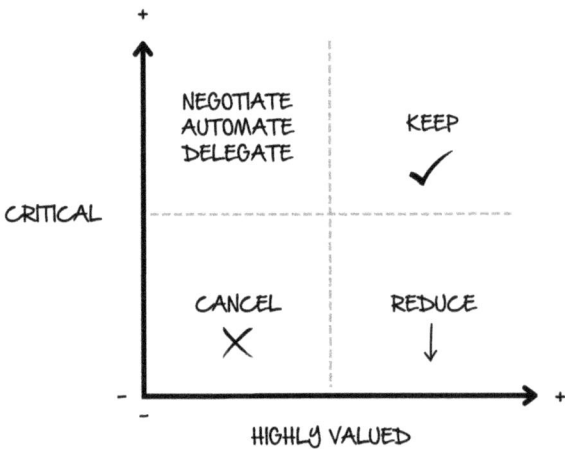

Prioritisation of expenses, part one

The critical things are going to be your survival living expenses. If you take a look at the image of Maslow's hierarchy of needs (below), you'll see that at the bottom you have your physiological needs: food, shelter, water. They're critical things.

Maslow's hierarchy of needs[28]

You need shelter, you need food, you need water, and you need cleaning products and medicines to stay healthy and have the best chance of survival. These expenses would be classed as critical. Unless you take care of these things, you have hard-wired limits that literally disable you from ascending to ever higher degrees of security, complexity and creativity.

This is why if you're trying to learn to trade before you have any savings or financial order, your situation will prevent you from being successful. That approach will stop you getting to where you want to

---

28   S McLeod, PhD, 'Maslow's Hierarchy Of Needs', Simply Psychology (14 March 2025), www.simplypsychology.org/maslow.html, accessed 15 April 2025

be because you cannot physically skip human evolutionary needs. More on that later.

The highly valued expenses are going to be more to do with what you or your family define as valuable. There will be certain expenses that fall under both categories. In the matrix above, the top right-hand quadrant is for expenses that are both highly valued and critical. An example might be your mortgage or rent. This expense is critical because you need shelter, but it might also fall under the category of highly valued because if you have no shelter or warmth, your standard of life is going to be pretty low. If you haven't got a roof over your head, you're going to struggle to live a very inspiring life. Any expenses in this quadrant, you are going to keep.

Critical but not valuable expenses will be things like insurance, taxes etc. These expenses are placed in the highly critical quadrant located in the top left-hand side of the matrix. Any expense in this quadrant, you are going to either negotiate as soon as you can, delegate to someone else to look after or automate via direct debit or standing order.

The bottom right-hand quadrant is for expenses that are highly valued, but not as critical. Such expenses might include family meals out. If that's how you and your family spend your quality time together and you really converse and bond over a nice meal at your favourite restaurant, that will be an expense that is valuable to you. It could also be something like going to the cinema, a gaming activity or a club to play or watch sports like skating, soccer or hockey etc. It could be a more selfish expense like massages, spa visits or beauty treatments. In other words, it's any expense that's highly valuable to you or your family, but not critical. Any expense placed in the bottom right-hand quadrant, you are going to try to reduce so that you can keep the value there while making savings.

Finally, the bottom-left quadrant is for non-critical and low-value expenses. You are simply going to prioritise cancelling these altogether. Just by doing this process, you'll likely be amazed at how many expenses fall into that category. So often, people buy stuff because someone else thinks it's good to have. They are simply accumulating expenses for status alone. My advice is to get rid of them.

So far in this process, you have highlighted hot spots in your expenses, identified critical and valuable expenses, prioritised the savings to be made by scoring them between 1–10 and cancelled any unnecessary outgoings. Some people struggle with the 1–10 prioritising process and get overwhelmed, so I am going to run you through another helpful matrix to help you understand the order in which you need to make the savings and prioritise them.

The matrix itself looks similar to the first one.

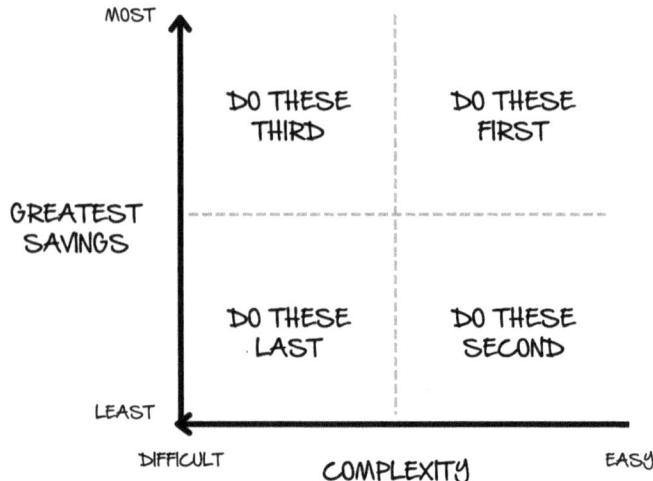

Prioritisation of expenses, part two

This time, the left-hand axis represents the savings from lowest to highest, and the bottom axis represents the complexity of making the saving.

Once you have recognised the hot spots or big unnecessary expenses, it makes sense to prioritise the greatest saving first. That's the expense that will involve the least complexity to make the biggest saving.

Some savings can be made simply by logging in to an online dashboard or app and clicking a few buttons. To make savings on other expenses, you may be required to book an appointment, travel to the bank or go through a credit search, which is a little more complex. Identify the expenses that offer the greatest savings with minimum complexity. Any expenses that fall under this category will be placed in the top right-hand quadrant of the matrix.

The bottom right-hand quadrant is for expenses that offer minimum savings with little complexity. In other words, you can still save some money and it's easy to do. My advice is to prioritise those savings second.

The top left-hand quadrant represents expenses that offer great savings, but they're made with a little more complexity. You are going to prioritise them third.

Finally, the bottom left-hand quadrant represents expenses that offer minimum savings for maximum complexity. You will do those last to avoid the risk of becoming demotivated.

Once you have completed this exercise, you will have a list of savings you can make in order of priority, and an idea of what savings you can gain from on each of your expenses. Next to each, write the current expense and the new expense once the savings have been made. Then add up all of the savings and write down the total.

Optimising your savings

Whenever I take people through this process, they are excited and amazed at just how much they have managed to save. Most of the time it's around a 10% saving, but I have had clients report savings of up to 75%.

It can be tempting to go and spend your newfound savings on consumables and luxuries, but the key here is to treat them as if you are still paying the expenses as they were. Instead of spending the savings on the old expenses, though, you are going to allocate that spare cash into investing in yourself. With the initial savings, you are firstly going to start building your cash buffer, then continue paying into it until you reach the buffer threshold you are satisfied with.

Once the buffer is filled, pay yourself the savings, but instead of spending the money on things that depreciate, spend it on self-development. There is an intangible income growth element when you invest in books, courses, masterminds, mentorships and boot camps. The new skills, ideas and strategies you learn from investing in your development will increase your knowledge and help you run your business (if you have one) more efficiently. You'll be able to make more sales, generate higher profit, learn a new money-making skill or start a side business.

The next thing to do is to write a list of all the things you could invest in that align with your values and interests. This will help you grow as a person so you naturally develop more income. Next to each investment, write the cost of it.

You could convert some of the savings on your expenses into a monthly audiobook membership that allows you to read a certain number of books on your favourite topics each month, for example. You might have your eye on a business workshop or retreat. Prioritise your list from 1–10 on how important those things are to you.

To hear me talk in more detail about optimising your savings on your expenses, go to www.alwaysfree.com/expenses.

Creating your wealth liquidity system

You have stopped the bleeding and been brave enough to stare your finances in the face. You have made some savings. You have built a cash buffer, and you may have ended up with a pot of cash to spend on self-development and income-growing endeavours.

The next step is to ensure you have an effective and sustainable system to allow your new financial habits to be maintained and harvested. This is where you start to build your wealth liquidity system.

Imagine you have crash landed on a deserted island in the middle of the Indian Ocean and it's swelteringly hot. You are alone and only have the debris from the wreckage of the aeroplane and the clothes on your back for shelter. Two days go by and you are so thirsty that you are hoping and praying for rain, when suddenly the sky clouds over. There is a rumble of thunder and a tropical storm opens up. Rain!

You open your mouth wide and stand there drinking for thirty minutes before it stops. The clouds disappear, the bright hot sunshine returns and you again have no certainty over when you might get another drink.

Imagine if you had spent the previous two days searching the debris of the aircraft for cases, containers, pots, pans, boxes, buckets, inflatable boats, cubicles, bottles and cups to catch as much of the falling rain as possible. Then you would have bought some time into the future.

The Three Buckets

I am going to show you a way to organise a series of allocations that will allow you to build the most powerful wealth liquidity system. A system that will organise, prioritise, grow and accelerate every single penny that you accumulate so you can achieve true financial freedom and live an inspired life in the shortest time period. It starts with the Three Buckets.

The Three Buckets are:

- Separate
- Coordinate
- Automate

Separate

We must keep a healthy body by having good food, shelter, water and clothing. We must have a healthy mind to enable us to expand our knowledge and thinking through observation, books, travel experiences and appreciation. We must do what we love to achieve true fulfilment through purpose and inspiration. If we cannot do what we love, we are in poverty.

I have seen people empower their mind by learning and learning and learning, only never to share or implement anything they have learned. They end up unrewarded and unfulfilled. I have seen people empower their body while doing a job they hate. This ends up with them being unrewarded and unfulfilled.

If you are to master your financial destiny and live an inspired life, you must consider all three requirements. Most people finance each from one account on a first-come-first-served basis, but if we are to grow sustainably as human beings, it makes perfect sense to separate each of these requirements and set an allocation of income so that each one gets what it needs.

The first allocation is purely for the body. At the base level of human survival, we need food, shelter, water, cleaning products, clothing. We need those LEs covered to service the body and keep it safe.

Your body allocation may also include your car, your travel and any other main expenses that you identified earlier on. Essentially, these are your living expenses.

The second allocation of cash needs to go towards your development as a human being. This involves improving your mind, your knowledge and your wisdom via books, courses, mentorships, boot camps and resources or experiences that empower you and allow you to grow. You must service the mind to step beyond the status quo and take control of your own destiny.

The third allocation is for your soul. Your purpose. Your true being. Your greater cause, your love and your legacy. This is your financial freedom allocation that will help you remain on the right course towards your most inspired life. It should be put towards what you would love to do every day forever.

This allocation will ensure you get to wake up each and every day choosing how you spend your time. Choosing to participate only in actions you love to do. Love finds its most natural and spontaneous expression in giving. Love is denied expression by poverty, so you must set an allocation towards your purpose.

The purpose or freedom allocation is going to be split into savings and investments. You may have heard the phrase 'pay yourself first', and usually, it is used to reference a savings account. The issue with a savings account is that it's difficult to comprehend the meaning and purpose of it beyond money. When I think about paying myself first, I am thinking about paying my true self. My purpose. Paying an allocation towards doing whatever I want to do most and a cause that is beyond just me and my material needs.

The reason it is so important to identify and separate each of these allocations is to differentiate yourself from the majority of the population. Most people have one allocation for their LAs and whichever requirement comes first each month gets the lion's share. There is no consistency, no discipline and no direction.

This is why most people end up with more life at the end of their money than money at the end of their life. They forget to pay themselves first while strategically expanding their mind and servicing their body. They don't have an account that's forever growing towards their freedom. As these people reach their later years, they find themselves in a situation where they have to hope that their children place more value on financial freedom than they have so that they can look after them in their old age. Otherwise, they end up working in a job until they drop.

Coordinate

Now that you understand the allocations, you must coordinate each one and bring the different requirements into a harmonious and efficient relationship.

This is where I will explain how much income to allocate to each requirement.

We will start with the freedom allocation, seeing as this is the 'pay yourself first' portion. I recommend allocating a minimum 10% of every post-tax penny to your freedom and inspiration. If you have saved on your expenses already, it's wise to start allocating a portion of those savings here that represent 10% of your income.

If you cannot manage 10% just yet, allocate what you can, but I recommend you try to force it to 10%. As soon as you get paid, 10% goes into the freedom allocation and it's out of sight, out of mind. You've paid yourself first and you don't touch that money or use it for any other allocation. I am going to explain more on the dynamics and the accelerated growth of this allocation later.

The second allocation is the development one, which goes towards empowering your mind through books, mentorships, experiences, courses, masterminds and boot camps. Here, you are essentially investing in your mind. I suggest you make this a non-negotiable 10%.

The most successful, profitable and long-lasting companies in the world invest around 10% of their revenue into research and development.[29] The reason

---

29 HJ Abolrous, 'Is your R&D spend healthy?' (RingStone, 14 November 2023), www.ringstonetech.com/post/is-your-r-d-spend-healthy, accessed 15 April 2025

they do this is to grow their revenue year-on-year. In your personal life, research and development is represented by investing in your wisdom and knowledge and empowering your mind. If the best minds and companies in the world are doing it, then it's wise for you to do it too.

Although this allocation may feel uncomfortable at first due to the intangibility element, you will soon realise that being around people who are going to push you, educate you, give you ideas and help to expand your mind is truly liberating. As you experience quantum leaps in your awareness and consciousness, you will rise up as a person.

Continuing to allocate 10% of your income into your development bucket will result in you meeting peers and mentors who will share ideas with you that will force you to elevate your game. If you can use the knowledge and new skills you gain to grow your income by just 10% per year, your entire liquidity system will accelerate, shaving years off your run to financial freedom.

The final allocation is going to be for the living expenses you need to maintain your lifestyle and service your body. This allocation is the remainder of the other two. The reason I refer to it as the remainder is because the purpose and freedom allocation is relative to the body allocation, with the mind allocation being fixed. For example, if you are initially allocating 9% to your freedom and 10% to your mind, then your allocation to your body will be 81%. If you subsequently allocate 10% to your freedom, along with the 10% to your mind, then your allocation to your body would be 80%.

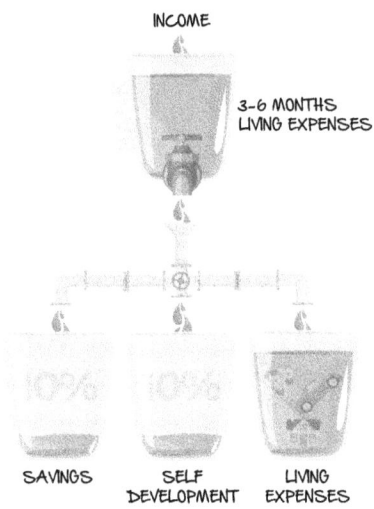

Automate

For most people, money causes fluctuations in emotions. Because of this, they tend to lack discipline and consistency when it comes to saving, spending and ultimately building wealth. This is why most people never achieve a level of financial freedom and stability.

I speak to many people who say they will start saving one day and it always seems to be tomorrow or in the future. If they do eventually start to save, they have no strategy because they are being driven by emotion. Emotions destroy wealth and strategies build wealth.

The thing is, time is of the essence. If you haven't started saving, then you need to do so. If you are already saving, then understand that every fourteen years, the value of your cash savings will halve due to inflation. This means that to maintain the lifestyle you have right now, in fourteen years' time you will need double the amount of money. If you are to build wealth and reach financial freedom efficiently, you need to remove emotions from the process.

Studies in behavioural economics have consistently shown that even small amounts of friction, such as requiring customers to manually renew a policy by writing a cheque or making a bank transfer, can lead to significant drop-offs in engagement. In contrast, automatic and seamless renewal processes tend to result in much higher retention rates. While specific figures vary across industries, the trend is clear: the easier you make it for someone to continue, the more likely they are to stay.

These types of studies indicate that whenever we remove emotions from the financial decision-making process by using automations, we move towards strategic planning instead of emotional turmoil. Strategies build wealth. If you rely on emotions to make your financial decisions instead of strategy, you will find that you never sustainably build wealth.

Now you understand the different allocations and the purpose of each one, we are going to remove emotion and replace it with strategy. We are going to build the first part of your wealth liquidity system.

It's likely that you have one primary personal bank account and every penny you earn gets transferred into that. Your income gets poured into your one account, and then spills out through the cracks in the bucket you recognised earlier. There are usually no allocations of any kind set up.

What I advise you to do is each and every time you get paid, you deplete the primary account into three sub-level accounts to cover the allocations we have just discussed. These sub-level bank accounts are going to be for the body, the mind and your purpose and freedom.

The next step is to automate the allocations with your bank. Each and every time you get paid, 10% will go into your mind account, where you will accumulate income to be spent on books, masterminds, courses, accelerators, boot camps and so on. Then you will have 10% of your income automatically allocated into your purpose and freedom account, which will be an ever-growing account accelerated by being diversified into investments. More on that later. Finally, the remainder of your income will get automatically transferred into your body or living account, which is where all of your LEs will be debited each month.

Physical automated bank accounts for your allocations will ensure that each requirement receives the correct portion of income you need to grow and reach financial freedom. Automated banking is by far the most underrated wealth creation strategy I have ever seen. It's the most powerful and reliable way to ensure you pay yourself first.

This automation structure is extremely easy to set up. With most digital online banks such as Monzo and Starling, the entire process to set up the account and sub-level accounts, as well as the automatic distributions and allocations, can take fewer than ten minutes to complete.

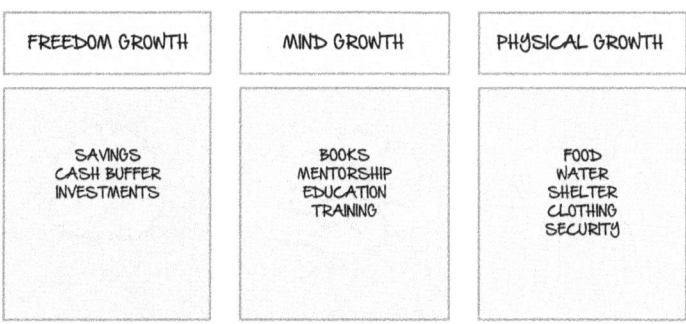

Income allocations

It should be noted that when it comes to the savings we talked about earlier, I recommend saving up a cash buffer of between three and six months' worth of living expenses as a minimum before you move to the next step of investing. However, with the self-development or mind account, I don't really have a limit, because sometimes there will be an accelerator programme that I want to take, sometimes I'll buy some books, and sometimes I'll attend a boot camp. Then there will be times that the funds will accumulate. Although I try to stay consistent, sometimes there are just no programmes, books or courses that interest me and so the account will build up. There have been other times where I have attended the same accelerator twice because I got so much value from it.

The point is, I disperse the self-development allocation as consistently and evenly as I can so that I am constantly improving my mind. I know there is an income growth element to doing so.

Reducing debt

At this point, I want to address a common objection that comes up regarding setting up the wealth liquidity system, and it is related to a subject we touched on earlier: debt.

People often believe it is better to wait until they are out of debt before they start to save. I have found that the habit of saving is the most important one you can develop. I have also found from studying people's spending behaviour and emotion that if they have a debt, as they start reducing it, they feel frivolous and instead of saving, they increase their debt again. This endless cycle stops them from ever making the decision to save.

Another objection I hear a lot of the time is, 'I don't earn enough to save yet' or 'When I get more money, I will start saving' or 'When I get a promotion...' or 'When my mortgage is paid off...' These are excuses for not placing a high value on wealth building and financial freedom. The people who say these things are under the illusion that the more they earn, the more disposable income they will have, which you now know is not statistically true.

Most of the time, insufficient income is not what is stopping people from saving; it's their priorities. You must pay yourself first. This means paying yourself before you pay the banks. If you are in debt, my advice is to build the habit of saving alongside paying down the debt and do them simultaneously rather than one at a time.

It is important that you are able to clear down non-cash-flow producing debt (as explained in Chapter 9) as soon as possible. If you have large debts, then it should be a priority to reduce and clear them, but still save and pay yourself too. If you can only afford to save £10 a month then start with £10. The habit of saving and giving yourself permission to focus on building an account that's forever growing towards your prosperity is more important than the actual amount.

I have spoken to people who take decades to pay off debt and I have also seen people clear debt very fast. From a combination of my studies in human psychology and witnessing the most effective strategies, I am going to share two methods of clearing debts as efficiently as possible.

Method 1: The Snowball Method[30]

This is a method created by finance expert Dave Ramsey and it has a tremendous success rate. It works by focusing on paying off debt in order from the smallest to largest and gaining momentum as you knock out each balance. You throw as much as you can at clearing the smallest debt while paying the minimum on the rest. Once the smallest debt is paid in full, you roll the money you were using for that debt into the next smallest balance, and so on.

As mentioned earlier, money is extremely emotive. The reason this strategy works so well is because it's all about behaviour modification. Dave Ramsey says, 'Winning at money is 80 percent behavior and 20 percent head knowledge.'[31] If you start paying down

---

30 G Kamel, 'How the debt snowball method works' (Ramsey Solutions, 14 August 2024), www.ramseysolutions.com/debt/how-the-debt-snowball-method-works, accessed 19 October 2024
31 D Ramsey, *The Total Money Makeover* (Nelson Current, 2009)

your student loan first because it's the largest debt, the chances are you won't clear it for a long time. You will see the numbers going down on the balance, but pretty soon, you will lose steam and stop paying extra. Why? Because it's taking forever to achieve your goal.

On top of that, you will still have all your small, annoying debts hanging around, but when you clear the smallest debt first, you see progress quickly. Then you will feel accomplished and hopeful. Once that debt is cleared, the second debt will follow, and then the next. When you see the plan working, you're more likely to feel you can stick it out, and then you'll succeed in becoming debt-free!

Method 2: The Avalanche Method

This is a more common and well-known approach to clearing debt with the focus being on paying down the debt with the highest interest first. With this payoff strategy, you make minimum monthly payments on all your other debts while paying extra towards your debt with the highest interest rate until it's gone.

The benefits of using this method are that you will pay less in interest and it will actually take less time to pay off your debts. However, the Snowball statistically has a higher success rate.[32] This goes to show

---

32 R Boyer, 'The "snowball approach" to debt', (Kellogg School of Management, 7 August 2012), www.kellogg.northwestern.edu/news_articles/2012/snowball-approach.aspx, accessed 15 April 2025

that when it comes to debt, we like to see progress and be able to tick 'complete' on a list. This is motivating and builds momentum.

The debt repayment strategy you choose will depend on your personality, your unique goals and feelings about debt. Saving money on interest is likely to be your main motivation if you have a lot of high-interest debt from things like credit cards and payday loans, so the Avalanche could be your better option. On the other hand, if you find it difficult to stay motivated and are looking for more immediate results, the Snowball may make more sense. The important part is to stick to your plan of committing to paying off your debt. Doing so will allow you to move faster towards your financial goals.

You can check which debt repayment method may suit you better by using my Debt Destroyer Tool© at www.alwaysfree.com/debt.

TOP TIP

When it comes to saving and taking control of your finances, the most uninspiring thing you can do is to save every penny you earn and forget to live and grow. For you to grow, money must flow in and out of your hands like a controlled current.

The more you hold on tightly to your money and don't let any leave you, the harder it is for cash to come into your grasp. Of course, if you go too far the other way, that's not wise either.

The key is to ease your grip a little bit so you can move more elegantly with money throughout your life.

13
Asset Accumulation

Getting rich slowly and methodically allows your psychology to keep up with the growth of your money. My Tiers of Freedom® process follows a path that is ordered a certain way because it's aligned with your own evolutionary order of needs.

Once you have built the foundation of the wealth liquidity system by controlling your living costs, structuring your income allocations and automating the process, you can now focus on growing your liquidity and wealth. The Tiers of Freedom® structure takes your current situation and provides you with the tools and strategies to focus on the components that allow you to achieve three objectives and become financially free.

It starts by focusing on accumulating appreciating assets that go up in value and provide a positive ROI, as opposed to buying depreciating assets. In short, you want to accumulate assets that are income generating.

The easiest way to think of this process is as a gradual levelling up. Each time you 'fill up' a level, you earn your way to move to the next one. This is all about your mind and ensuring that you take on additional risk bit by bit, thereby remaining calm and not jeopardising your returns out of fear. This is why you can't jump straight to trading. You have to earn your stripes if you want to see sustainable long-term success.

There are several stages to this process which I have broken into four parts.

Part I – Cash buffer comforts

The oldest part of our brain is the amygdala.[33] From an evolutionary standpoint, it is essentially responsible for keeping us safe. Our animal instinct doesn't like change and it certainly doesn't like risk. It's very reactive and it wants to make sure we have the best chance of survival in the immediate future.

---

33 G Rayner, 'The emotion centre is the oldest part of the human brain: Why mood is so important' (The Conversation, 25 September 2016), https://theconversation.com/the-emotion-centre-is-the-oldest-part-of-the-human-brain-why-is-mood-so-important-63324#, accessed 21 October 2024

When people live hand to mouth and spend more than they earn each month, they are constantly triggering the amygdala because if they don't have stable financial security, there is a chance that the basic human needs, ie food, shelter, warmth etc, will be at risk. An important part of accumulating wealth is to keep this part of your brain stable so you can focus on making better decisions that are guided by your inner self instead of scarcity, needy desperation or trying to make quick returns. The best way to do this is to save a cushion of cash that is kept in your account to cover you should something drastically affect your income tomorrow. Having a pot of liquid cash sitting there as a buffer will keep the amygdala from going into survival mode and instead open up the growth part of your brain to explore, create and innovate.

Work out what it costs you to have food, shelter, clothing, water and security each month and make a commitment to save enough liquid cash to cover these expenses for at least three months should you lose your income tomorrow. The more time you can survive into the future, the better.

In 2023, the UK entered a recession following one of the most impactful pandemics in history. Businesses were forced to close after the majority of the population had been forced into a lockdown situation and globally, social dynamics shifted radically. We witnessed some of the country's largest companies go into liquidation and saw thousands of small businesses dissolve.

One in ten restaurants closed their doors forever[34] and thousands of people became unemployed.[35]

The pandemic opened everyone's eyes to the importance of having liquid cash cushions in place. As everything came to a grinding halt, banks initially stopped lending money, estate agents closed and the housing market stalled. People who had no savings couldn't borrow money. They couldn't liquidate equity in their properties. They couldn't sell goods.

At this point, whoever had enough saved to cover their living costs would survive as normal and whoever had the longest period of living costs saved had the greatest chance of coming out the other side while keeping a level mind. Only businesses that had cash cushions covering months of operating costs into the future would survive this extraordinary situation.

Your cash buffer must be a priority. If you made savings on your expenses or you earned some cash from selling off unused items, stash as much of that as you can into your cash buffer before you do anything else. My advice is to save a cash buffer of three months' worth of living expenses as soon as you can.

---

34   L Hooker, 'Covid: A tenth of Britain's restaurants lost during pandemic' (BBC News, 16 May 2021), www.bbc.co.uk/news/business-57087070, accessed 21 October 2024
35   A Powell, B Francis-Devine, H Clark, 'Coronavirus: Impact on the labour markets' (House of Commons Library, 9 August 2022), https://researchbriefings.files.parliament.uk/documents/CBP-8898/CBP-8898.pdf, accessed 21 October 2024

You will then start to think more freely. You won't be frantically changing your strategy in business or chasing shiny objects. You will remain calm and poised. Having a cash buffer opens your mind to opportunities and you see the world in a different way. It's liberating.

You can focus on your business, your job, your relationships, your partnerships, your health and your social life in a way that allows you to grow, which in turn naturally starts to accelerate your income too. You become more caring, more creative and more free. You feel in control and you certainly make more sensible spending decisions.

With that in mind, the first asset you are going to accumulate is a cushion of cash savings that equals a multiplication of your monthly living expenses. Start with three months, but aim for twelve.

The most profitable businesses on Earth carry an average of nine to twelve months of operating costs in liquid cash at any one time.[36] The more you have, the more abundant you feel.

Cash buffer goals:

- Three to six months = essential
- Six to nine months = great
- Nine to twelve months = ideal

---

36 Figure based on publically available information from finance sites and company earnings reports.

This is the first asset to focus on accumulating.

Immediate ROI on the cash buffer

If you are wondering whether having what feels like a large amount of cash just sitting in the bank doing nothing is the best course of action, my answer is *yes*!

Commonly, people think that not investing that much cash is a waste, but they are missing the point. The cash buffer is there to relieve the animal brain (amygdala) as we know that we can access it at any point because it's liquid and it is not at risk in any way. For that reason, there is an immediate ROI to simply having the cash buffer sitting in a bank account.

Let me explain…

Imagine I am a builder who has absolutely no cash buffer and I have just completed some work on your new home extension. Upon completion, you call me up and explain that you have found some snags with the work and would like them resolved before paying my final bill.

My reaction is likely to be aggressive. Knowing that I need that money if I'm going to eat, I will huff and puff and complain, which will result in you not employing me again, not recommending me to anyone, and possibly not paying me the full amount owed.

Now let's rewind a bit and imagine I had a six-month cash buffer. That would mean I had peace of mind that if I didn't receive the money from you today, I could live for six months before having to worry about paying for food, shelter etc. My attitude would be completely different.

Instead of being aggressive and defensive, I would say something like, 'Don't worry, I am going to ensure all the snags are seen to and the job is done to the standard of your expectations. I want to ensure we build a long-lasting relationship together and it is in my interest to make sure you are happy with my services.' If I approach you with this tone and mentality, the chances are that you will employ me again, give me a tip, recommend me to all your friends and colleagues, and because I don't need immediate money, I can charge more, knowing that people will gladly pay it for the service they receive.

Let me reiterate the purpose and importance of having the cash buffer sitting in the bank doing nothing: it is to allow your creative, innovative and loving brain to come alive so you can get out of scarcity and obscurity and let more income flow to you naturally. You will be more focused at your job, in your business, with your partner, in your relationships, in your health, and every area of your life will see the benefits of having the cash buffer safely stored in liquidity.

If you are worried about getting a better return, put it in a high-interest savings account, but cash is just fine. Get your cash buffer in place!

Forced Accelerated Savings Technique (FAST)®

When it comes to saving, although setting aside 10% of your income is good, it's still an incomplete strategy for exponential wealth and prosperity. Yes, your income will inevitably grow exponentially if you invest 10% of every penny earned into developing your mind, and that will increase the savings amount, but it's still a relatively linear way to manage savings.

What I am about to explain to you, if implemented, will have a compound effect on your savings, your liquidity, your net worth and your lifestyle. Just bolting on this strategy turns saving money into a wealth acceleration machine.

Once you have set up and automated the savings allocation, the key is to ramp up the savings four times per year using the Forced Accelerated Savings Technique (FAST):

- **F**orced
- **A**ccelerated
- **S**avings
- **T**echnique

Every quarter, the goal is to increase the savings allocation by 10% by logging on to your banking platform and increasing the automated deposit. For example:

- Month 1: 10%
- Month 4: 11%
- Month 7: 12.1%
- Month 10: 13.3%
- Month 13: 14.6%
- Month 16: 16.1%

And so on.

This strategy has two main benefits to accelerating wealth. Firstly, it will allow you to double your savings approximately every twenty-four months. Secondly, it forces you to put a demand on your lifestyle and creativity.

The key is to keep increasing your savings to the border of discomfort. I have found that the sweet spot for doing this is every three months. After ninety days, you have started to acclimatise to the allocation before increasing it again.

If you have ever decided to make a purchase that is outside your comfort zone, such as a new car or house, you will know that at first, you feel slightly uneasy about the payments and wonder how you are going to afford them. After three months, you acclimatise to the new monthly expense. When you push to the edge of your comfort zone, you naturally look for and attract opportunities to help you out. You get more business, a pay rise, a tax rebate, a new client.

There have been times in the past when I have gone to increase my savings, and by doing so have put myself in the position where I would not have been able to afford my savings the following quarter if I didn't reduce my living costs or make more income. Instead of deciding not to ramp up my savings, I looked for and found new opportunities, for example I would sell a batch of programmes. If you look, you too will find ways to increase your income when you commit.

This technique falls down when people get tempted to splurge surplus money on things that are not beneficial for wealth building and financial freedom, such as depreciating consumables. Instead of doing that, go and increase your savings to tighten up your wealth liquidity system and put a demand on yourself.

Once you cross the threshold of saving 50% of every penny you make in income, the time it takes to reach financial independence is significantly reduced. You also feel more prosperous. You see more opportunities. You play life at a different level.

Finally, although increasing your savings will be a manual process of logging on to your banking platform, you want to remove as much emotion as possible, so my advice is to set a reminder in your calendar on the first of every quarter month. As soon as the reminder alarm goes off, log in to your bank and do it straight away.

As you work through each stage of the book, you'll earn a Tiers of Freedom Badge. Having finished this section, you have now earned your first Tiers of Freedom Bedrock Badge! You have a full understanding of how to build a solid wealth foundation and my hope is that you implement what you have learned so far.

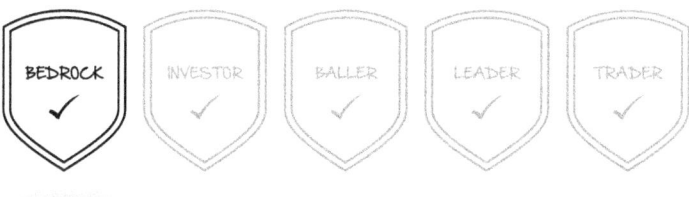

Part II – Investing to grow your wealth

Although it's wise to have your cash buffer saved, it's sensible to put anything you save over and above that into assets that will outperform the inflation rate to allow your wealth to grow.

The average inflation rate in the UK over the last twenty-five years has been approximately 2.8% per year.[37] This means that every penny that sits in your bank account loses 2.8% in value annually. To break

---

37 'UK public inflation expectations fall to lowest in over 2 years', *Financial Times* (15 March 2024), www.ft.com/content/a05462e1-529d-42dc-9919-cb4911b596d6, accessed 15 April 2025

even with inflation, you must generate at least a 2.8% return after tax on your money. This shows why it's wise to start investing your surplus cash savings into assets that will outperform the inflation rate.

At this point, some people think that to invest, they have to have studied economics and have a degree in finance. Instead of discovering how to invest their money properly, they have a desire to take their spare cash, open a trading account and speculate to accumulate the highest return possible in the shortest amount of time, thinking that is 'investing'.

This approach is usually down to lack of knowledge and understanding. It's also often correlated to an infatuation with making big money, which can be motivated by a resentment towards a person's current job, financial situation or levels of debt. This is a risky strategy driven by emotion, which is why the system I am teaching you is in a specific order.

While it's fairly natural to want the most bang for your buck, you must focus on sustainability and probabilities. We have talked about building the psychological foundations by getting your mindset right and having a cash buffer in place before putting any money at risk. I want you to think about your investments the same way. You want to build a pyramid with a solid foundation and a strong structure that will stand the tests of time.

ASSET ACCUMULATION

The way to build wealth is to think of the different tiers of the pyramid as locked until you earn the right to unlock them.

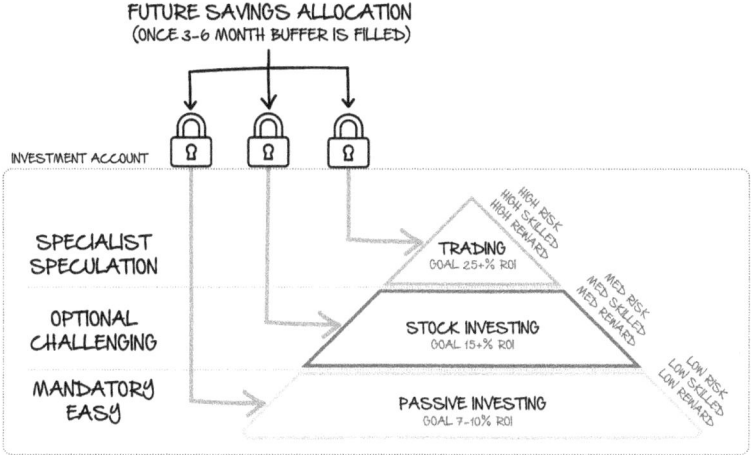

Tier 3 is the lowest tier. This is going to be where you store the majority of your liquidity to strengthen your foundations. It is the most passive, the easiest to set up, requires the least skill and therefore carries the lowest form of risk.

Tier 2 requires more skill and more time to manage, and is therefore more risky than Tier 3. Once unlocked, this tier yields better returns if you do what I am going to show you.

Then, of course, there is Tier 1 at the top of the pyramid. This tier requires the most time and skill to unlock, and therefore is the riskiest. It is also extremely volatile. Most people fail to generate consistent returns because they simply do not earn the right to unlock this tier at the right time.

Now let's focus on growing and accelerating your wealth in a way that allows you to live the life you want without sacrificing longevity and sustainability. People often become infatuated with hearing about how someone got lucky and made a huge ROI, but what you usually find is that they end up giving it back to the market because they haven't built a solid foundation. I want you to think about your investment account as a solid and strong pyramid structure. If you want to build sustainable wealth and reach financial freedom as efficiently as possible, my advice is to save, invest, then speculate. See the following investment account example.

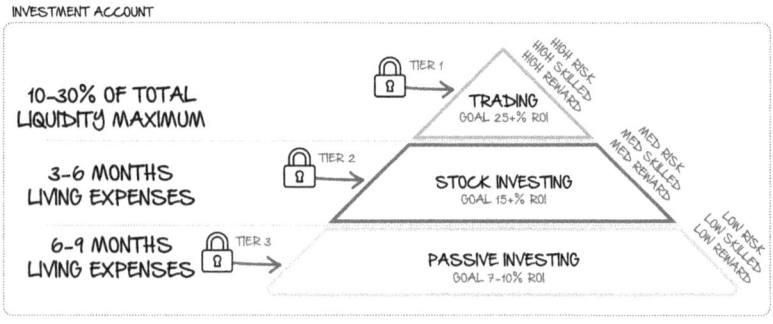

Once your cash buffer of living expenses is filled, you can consider an investing framework in which to deposit future monthly savings allocations. The framework I am about to share with you is what I have found to be the most efficient. This investing structure allowed me to replace my income completely within 3.5 years.

The key investments I will be explaining are:

- **Investing passively.** Automation of building a buffer and buying the market (create a portfolio that tracks the market performance) – Tier 3.
- **Investing in stocks.** Analysing and picking individual stocks – Tier 2.
- **Speculation.** Allocating a portion of you investment account to trading – Tier 1.

Each of these will serve a unique purpose in your wealth building and when combined will allow you to maximise returns, be highly rewarded and stay fulfilled.

Investment structure

Once you have your living expense buffer saved in pure liquid cash, you can open up the tap on your savings bucket and bypass all future surplus savings (other than your living expense buffer) into an investment account.

ALWAYS FREE

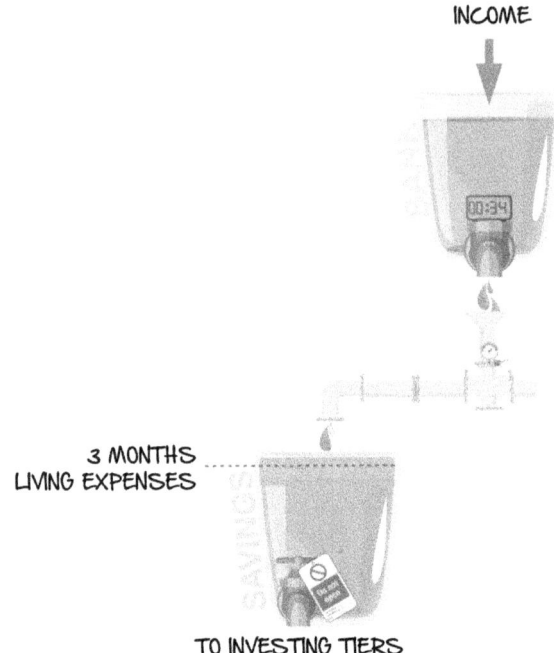

Before we get into the actual strategies and assets, it's important you understand the most powerful way to structure your investments so that you know the order, the purpose and the relationship between them all. How you put your money to work is going to have varying levels of risk, time requirement, skill, effort and returns.

The investment account structure should look like the diagram below.

ASSET ACCUMULATION

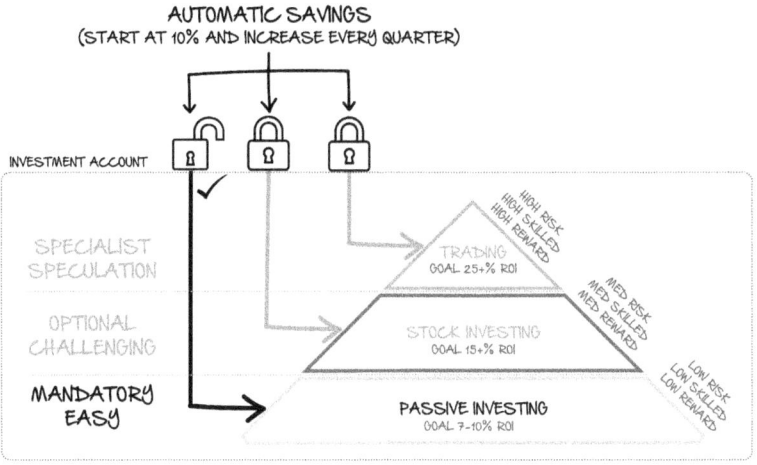

As you can see, each of the tiers is locked. The bottom tier (Tier 3) is unlocked once the living expense buffer is filled. Once unlocked, this part of your investment account is going to be extremely passive. It should take no longer than an hour of your time to set up and automate payments into this account. This tier will produce returns consistently over time on a set-and-forget basis.

The middle tier (Tier 2) is unlocked when you have reached a buffer of cash in the lowest tier plus some surplus liquidity from your savings allocations that you can use to invest into stocks. This is known as value investing. Although it's a little riskier than the lowest tier, it's still not going to be overly complex, and because you have built additional cash cushions, you aren't at risk of activating your animal brain and jeopardising the entire system. This tier is also not going to be overly time consuming.

Finally, there is the upper tier, which we're calling Tier 1. This tier gets unlocked once you have an additional buffer of cash working for you in the middle tier and surplus liquidity from your saving allocations to invest here.

Tier 1 is for pure speculation and trading. In other words, short-term gains from using skill to exploit supply and demand in different markets like the financial markets, indices, futures and stocks, through to less liquid speculative vehicles such as property, fine wine, art, classic cars, watches etc.

This section of the investment pyramid is known as zero sum. You are essentially learning a skill and using it to beat other contenders in the marketplace by trading – buying underpriced assets from fearful sellers and selling overpriced assets to greedy buyers. This tier is much higher risk and, depending on the asset class or the market, there is going to be a higher price for entry too.

If you were to invest 10% of your income into Tier 3 and accelerate your savings every three months, this alone would be an extremely powerful wealth creation strategy. With compounding, you would likely replace your current income within a ten to fifteen year period.

If you activate Tier 2, you want to be looking at returns over 15% on average. With Tier 1, you want to be aiming for returns of 25% minimum to really make it worth the time and effort.

You can unlock one, two or all three of these tiers. The lower tier is considered income, the middle tier is considered balance and the higher tier is considered speculation. If you master all three, you will have the most acceleration in your returns, but my advice is to start with Tier 3, build a cushion, and then maybe do some stock picking in Tier 2. Once you've reached this stage, build another cushion, and then finally go into speculation if that is something you desire with what your life looks like at that point. Depending on your agenda, you can dynamically modulate the ratio of the allocation in the entire portfolio between the three tiers.

You might decide to allocate 90% of your investment liquidity into the lower tier and 10% into the middle tier. If you decide to refine your trading skills, you might put 80% into the lower tier, 15% into the middle tier and 5% into Tier 1. If you get really good at trading, you may even have a ratio of 50% into Tier 1 and 40/10 into passive investments and stocks. It really will depend on what your goals are at that point in time. I frequently move money around my investment accounts depending on my motivations.

This is an overview of the investment account structure. Remember, if you only do Tier 3, that's absolutely fine. You can just let that run for years and it will accelerate your journey to financial independence, but if you manage to master all three, your run to financial independence is going to be considerably faster.

You are probably thinking, 'Great, but what do I invest in?' We are going to cover the different tiered strategies now.

Start by generating consistent returns through passive investing in Tier 3. This is foundational and carries the lowest risk. Don't be tempted to jump to Tier 1 before you have earned your right to invest at that level.

Part III – Earning your right to risk

I am fascinated by brain and neurological research. I have already mentioned the amygdala and understand that this most primitive part of the brain functions from an 'all-or-none' or stimulus response.

The brain stem has a little more refinement. This means you have more control over your responses. Then when you get into the limbic part of the brain, you get more control still. In the cortex, there is even more control, and by the time you reach the upper level of your brain, the corpus colosseum, you have maximum associations and responses instead of reflexes.

However, under stress, the amygdala takes over and you tend to react in an all-or-none way. There may have been times where you were in rage, and it was like you could see yourself acting out, but couldn't do anything about it. This is a reflex from the animal part of your brain.

Because the refined parts of the brain are poised and the primitive parts are reactive, it is when we are reactive that it's most important that we have our finances stable and taken care of. When we are poised, we can handle volatility because that's when we are least likely to react.

You can only handle stress if you know how to balance your perceptions and not be reactive to volatile fluctuations. Although technically, higher rewards come with higher risk, speculation often has a low return rate due to the fact people approach it before they have earned the right to risk. Earning this right allows your brain to handle the fluctuations and deal with the complexities of speculation.

It might be tempting to dive straight into trading and speculation, but to effectively navigate high volatility and complex investments, your mind must be calm and disciplined. The more mentally stable you are, the more external uncertainty you can handle without falling into emotional decision-making.

Research in behavioural economics shows that humans tend to become emotionally reactive when experiencing financial gains or losses—particularly under conditions of stress or uncertainty. While there isn't a universal threshold, studies on loss aversion and volatility intolerance suggest that even modest fluctuations in financial value can trigger cognitive and emotional stress responses.

A commonly observed pattern is that individuals can generally tolerate modest losses—around 10% of their liquid capital—without major psychological disruption. For example, if you had £100,000 and lost £10,000, you might feel uncomfortable, but your decision-making capacity would likely remain intact. However, larger losses often increase anxiety, trigger irrational behaviour, and impair judgment.

Interestingly, the concept of tithing in some religious traditions—asking for 10% of income—is thought to reflect a similar psychological threshold. It's just enough to feel meaningful, but not so much that it causes resistance or emotional instability.

The same logic applies in the opposite direction. A consistent gain of 10% feels rewarding yet manageable. But an unexpected windfall followed by a sudden drop in income can create emotional turbulence. We are more likely to remain poised and balanced when our financial gains and losses are gradual and predictable rather than extreme and erratic.

To develop a less chaotic mind to deal with complexities in the world such as volatile markets, speculation and investing, you must first earn your right to risk your capital at varying degrees of speculation. A wise strategy when starting out would be not to put more than 10% of your net worth or savings into passive investments. Then, when you start to invest in stocks, don't put more than 10% of the amount you have in passive investments into individual stocks. Finally, if you decide to speculate, do not put more than 10% of the value of your stock liquidity into trading.

Of course, these allocations can change the more you earn your right to risk and the more seasoned you become as an investor. We will cover this later; for now, just be aware there is an evolutionary comfort zone which fears the loss of more than 10% of anything. If you are to put your money to work in high levels of speculation, you are going to have to earn your way there.

As you build the wealth liquidity system in the order set out in this book, you actually become smarter and earn higher levels of risk by unlocking parts of the brain that can deal with high degrees of complexity. The most primitive parts of the brain are binary, meaning that they look for yes or no answers. As you calm these parts with certainty, you unlock the higher parts of your brain that have the ability to deal with multiple equations.

Earning your right to higher degrees of risk is not an idea, it's a science. If you do it in the wrong order, you will waste years of your life.

Types of risk

Before you put your money at risk, it is crucial to understand what the risks are. The key thing to remember here is to never let your money grow at a rate your mindset cannot keep up with. If you do so, you will not be able to keep the surplus. You will squander it.

There are varying levels of risk from passive investments through to speculative investments, so if you are going to consider using all three tiers, it's also wise to understand the difference between an investor and a speculator. An investor is defined as a person who commits capital into a portfolio over the long term with the expectation of financial returns that grow their money and/or provide an income from the return. A speculator is a person who actively trades markets with a higher-than-average risk for a shorter-than-average time horizon, all with the purpose of generating a higher-than-average profit potential.

The majority of retail traders (a retail trader is someone who trades using their own money) tend to be in the category of speculators, not investors. For this reason, the majority of them do not make money over time and they certainly do not outperform the market after broker fees.

This is why I recommend that you avoid becoming a pure 100% speculator, at least until your speculative returns exceed buying the market over an extended period of time. In other words, dilute your speculative

Tier 1 trading capital with longer-term passive investments from Tier 3 to stabilise the volatility of your overall portfolio. I will be talking about this in detail later.

Before we get to that, I will explain the main types of risk when you're investing into the market and how you can apply diversification to minimise capital at risk as well as increasing the probability of positive returns.

Company risk

Let's say you purchase shares in a 'well-performing' technology company that has been making huge innovations in wireless networking. As an investor, you ask yourself, what are all of the factors that could negatively impact this investment? The list might include company financials, marketing, cash-flow management, shareholder disagreements, performance of technology, price and profit margins, poor management and leadership, bankruptcy…

Buying into any one stock (one company in this example) exposes you to huge volatility. If you pick a winner, you can generate a nice return, but if you get it wrong, you could lose your entire investment. Unless you really know what you're doing, individual stock picking is a form of speculation that most rookies falsely mistake for investing.

This method is essentially having all of your eggs in one basket. If the company fails, you lose your money.

Sector risk

Let's say that instead of putting all your eggs into one basket and investing in one technology company, you invest in five different companies that are all innovating in wireless technology. For this example, you invest £5,000 into the five different companies. Four of them could go bankrupt and you would still have liquidity working for you.

This is called diversification, but it comes at a price. If four of the technology companies go bankrupt and one increases to ten times its original valuation, your total investment doesn't actually increase ten-fold. Rather, you 'only' double your total investment.

Here is what your £5,000 investment might look like over those five companies in a diversified example:

- Tech Company 1 (£1,000 of stock) – collapses
- Tech Company 2 (£1,000 of stock) – collapses
- Tech Company 3 (£1,000 of stock) – collapses
- Tech Company 4 (£1,000 of stock) – collapses
- Tech Company 5 (£1,000 of stock) – increases 1,000% (10 times)
- Total initial investment £5,000 – increases to £10,000

If you'd put the entire £5,000 investment into Tech Company 5, you could have turned it into £50,000, but through diversification, you reduced your downside risk at the cost of upside potential. If you had put the entire £5,000 investment into any individual company other than Tech Company 5, you would have lost every penny.

If you diversify across five different companies as opposed to just one, you are more likely to build sustainable wealth. However, what if the technology sector takes a hit overall?

Although you have diversified across multiple companies, you are still vulnerable to one sector. You could invest in fifty technology companies, but if there were a tsunami or an explosion at one of the major production plants from which multiple companies source or manufacture their equipment, then the entire sector could take a major hit. This is where it would be wise to diversify your investments across multiple companies *and* multiple sectors.

A wise investor implements sector diversification on top of company diversification. This means owning multiple stocks in pharmaceuticals, energy, telecoms, finance, health care, industrials, agriculture, information technology, real estate and utilities.

You might be thinking, 'If I have to buy into 50 companies in 10 different sectors, that's 500 companies! How would I be able to manage that?'

The answer is index funds.

Index funds are powerful stand-alone investment tools, and when combined with wise asset class diversification, they can form a passive investment portfolio that literally rivals the returns of many institutional hedge funds. An index fund is a group of companies that have been hand selected based on performance by some of the brightest financial minds on the planet. All of the hard work has been done for you.

A fund like the S&P 500 is a single investment that exposes you to a diversified variety of the top 500 companies in the world. These 500 companies are selected by a respected committee under strict guidelines, and are regularly tweaked and updated to remove underperforming companies when stronger alternatives arise.

Just like sports leagues, each quarter during the earnings report – a financial document released by public companies – the index fund companies are assessed and the worst performers get put in a relegation zone to be potentially booted out to make way for the better performing companies. This is a continuous process that ensures the fund grows. The growth is a result of the best business minds working together to innovate, solve problems and create solutions for billions of people around the globe. These companies are diversified across all sectors too.

If you are looking for a way to dilute and spread risk across your investments while still being able to invest in the best-performing companies, an index fund would be a wise choice. They are also extremely low cost. You can access a fund like this by purchasing a single instrument on nearly any brokerage platform with an expense ratio as low as 0.08%. That means for every £100,000 you invest, you could pay as little as £80 in fees for exposure to the index.

To give you some perspective, if you were to invest £100,000 in a property, not only would you be investing the cash into a non-liquid asset, but if you were to sell the property and realise the profit, the fees of an estate agent and solicitor would be more like 2–3%. This means you would be paying £2,000–£3,000 in fees for that investment instead of £80.

I believe that the most reliable, sustainable and scalable form of creating financial wealth is through service to humanity. Solving problems for other people via creative and innovative products and services in fair exchange for financial remuneration is the essence of the monetary system as we know it. By investing in stock index funds, you're investing in the most effective problem-solvers on Earth. Serving others is a staple of human fulfilment and business success. Stock index funds are well worth consideration in your financial independence strategy.

One point to note: buying into an index fund is different to buying individual stocks. If you buy the S&P 500, it includes Google, Microsoft, Apple and Facebook. However, just because that index contains those companies, it doesn't mean you would go out and buy stocks in each individually because they could be overvalued. The strategy for buying individual stocks is not the same as the strategy for buying into an index fund.

Asset risk

Even the top 500 companies listed on the top stock exchanges don't collectively go up in value every year. To smooth the equity curve and reduce any volatility further, you can consider adding a balance of differing assets such as commodities and bonds to your portfolio. This can ensure you limit your exposure to stock market risk while retaining the majority of the upside.

Your equity curve is a visual representation of the growth of your account in your investment portfolio. Ideally, you want this to be smooth (like a bell curve) rather than jagged and fluctuating up and down.

Billionaire hedge fund manager Ray Dalio of Bridgewater Associates created an 'All Seasons' strategy back in 1996.[38] It was designed and optimised

---

38 T Robbins, *Money Master The Game: 7 Simple Steps to Financial Freedom* (Simon & Schuster, 2014)

to deliver consistent passive returns in all market environments with low fluctuations and volatility.

The key components and weights of this strategy are:

- 30% in US stocks
- 40% in long-term US Treasury Bonds
- 15% in intermediate-term US Treasury Bonds
- 7.50% in gold
- 7.50% in broad commodity basket

In the last twenty years, a portfolio of this allocation has been back tested to produce an average annual return of between 7–9% (net of fees).[39] Over almost a forty-year period with the majority of those being profitable, the worst performing year was following the global financial crash, which saw returns of −3.74% regardless of the market dropping by −37%. When we speak about reaching a level of financial freedom whereby you can have a sum of investment capital working for you at low risk with a fixed-income return, this is it.

It should be noted that past performance is never a promise or guarantee of future returns. The purpose of mentioning this strategy is to give you an example

---

39 Lazy Portfolio Etf, 'Ray Dalio All Weather Portfolio: ETF allocation and returns' (no date), www.lazyportfolioetf.com/allocation/ray-dalio-all-weather, accessed 15 April 2025

of asset risk. We will be talking more about different asset classes and instruments later on in the speculation section. This is simply a general recommendation to look into the power of passive portfolio management using a diversified asset allocation such as All Seasons. I did not invent this asset allocation nor am I the original discoverer or pioneer of it. For this reason, I would encourage you to broaden your knowledge on this strategy by visiting www.bridgewater.com.

Another simplified strategy recommended by Warren Buffett is what is commonly known as the 90/10 strategy. When asked in an interview how he would like his estate to be managed and distributed when he died, Buffett replied, 'My advice to the trustee could not be more simple: put 10% of the cash in short-term government bonds and 90% in a very low-cost S&P 500 index fund… I believe the trust's long-term results from this policy will be superior to those attained by most investors – whether pension funds, institutions, or individuals – who employ high-fee managers.'[40]

When it comes to the most powerful investment strategies on Earth, they usually work in favour of maximum simplicity. Don't be fooled into thinking that to generate consistent returns and build tremendous

---

40 J Pan, 'After he dies, Warren Buffett says 90% of his wife's inheritance will go into this one investment — and it's not Berkshire Hathaway. Here's why, plus 1 extra tool to transfer wealth' (Yahoo! Finance, 3 March 2024), https://finance.yahoo.com/news/warren-buffett-says-dies-90-133400915.html, accessed 21 October 2024

wealth, you have to be a master of complex investment algorithms. That is a common misconception.

Here's a quick note on the reality of investing. According to performance data, the Vanguard S&P 500 Index Fund has recorded an average annual return of approximately 10.33% over the past thirty years.[41] This is a higher long-term return than the All Weather strategy, but the volatility is significantly greater. For example, in 2008 during the global financial crisis, the S&P 500 fell by −37.0%.[42] (Investopedia, 2023). In comparison, the All Weather Portfolio experienced much smaller drawdowns, such as −3.93% in its worst year, offering a smoother ride for investors seeking stability.

Any frustration you feel from taking the time to learn wise asset class diversification now will prepare you for dealing with the frustration of 30–40% drawdown years every now and then. Even in passive investing, you cannot completely escape work and effort.

Time risk

Even a balanced portfolio made up of multiple companies, sectors and asset classes will go through periods

---

[41] Lazy Portfolio Etf, 'Vanguard S&P 500 (VOO): Historical returns' (31 March 2025), www.lazyportfolioetf.com/etf/vanguard-sp-500-voo, accessed 15 April 2025

[42] JB Maverick, 'S&P 500 average returns and historical performance' (Investopedia, 26 December 2024), www.investopedia.com/ask/answers/042415/what-average-annual-return-sp-500.asp, accessed 15 April 2025

of growth and decline. This equity oscillation can (and often does) cause an emotional reaction that turns a long-term passive investor into a short-term active speculator who tries to time the market and maximise returns. However, it's essential that you don't confuse investing with trading.

Please understand the objective of Phase 2 of your financial freedom strategy is to create a highly stable passive financial foundation to complement your active speculation portfolio. Therefore, in your passive investment portfolio, you must transcend the notion of timing the market, which is why these strategies are in a certain order.

To transcend the obsession with market timing, ignore the urge to buy low and sell high. Rather, your investments must approximate the mean of the market.

You approximate the mean by investing the same amount at consistent time intervals. This is also called dollar cost averaging or pound cost averaging. By purchasing equal pound quantities of stocks, bonds or commodities at regular time intervals, sometimes you buy below the mean and sometimes you buy above the mean, but by consistently adding to your portfolio on a regular schedule, you will enable your net entry price ultimately to approximate the true mean over time.

By contrast, in active speculation and trading (which is the final tier of our pyramid), you do not want to:

- Approximate the mean
- Add to positions based on time intervals
- Average down your net entry price by adding to positions that move against you

Please refuse the temptation of mixing long-term passive investment strategies with short-term active speculation strategies. They are two completely different beasts that require two completely different approaches.

When it comes to long-term passive investment strategies, choose an interval that suits your income and savings schedule, and stick to it. By adding to your portfolio in equal pound quantities at even time intervals, you're not timing the market. Rather, your net entry price approximates the mean of the underlying market. This is what we refer to as 'time diversification' and it acts as the fourth dimension of portfolio diversification.

For a lasting perspective here, if you had timed the market perfectly following the global financial crash of 2008 and started investing at the lowest dip, you would have generated a positive return if you were still invested today. However, if you had started investing just before the crash at regular monthly intervals, not only would you still have a positive return, you would have more money in your investment account today than if you had waited until the crash.

Having skin in the game via consistent regular deposits allows you to fully exploit time diversification and cost averaging, which in turn allows you to approximate the mean growth of the market.

In summary, diversify across not only different companies, but also industries. Index funds are powerful stand-alone investment tools that you can use to diversify efficiently.

Part IV – Intelligent investing

By now, you have probably realised the importance of building a wealth system the right way, starting with low risk, then earning your way to greater degrees of risk. Now you have been introduced to index funds and some passive investing, I want to explain how this is all going to piece together in reality. This is how you will start filling up your investment account bucket.

As you fill up your investment account bucket, you can activate each of the tiers when your surplus cash cushions allow you to, while earning your right to risk. There are different levels of time, skill and risk required at all three tiers of the investment account. The idea is that the foundational tier (Tier 3) is considered income, the middle tier (Tier 2) is balance and the top tier (Tier 1) is growth. While you do not have to utilise any of them, you will benefit from maximum growth while retaining stability if you use all three.

Here's how to fill your investment account bucket up correctly so you can maintain stability and growth. Once the cash buffer is at the desired level of living expenses, the automation of savings doesn't stop. Instead, it gets transferred into Tier 3, which is a physical passive investment account like Vanguard. The account will then allocate your deposit to the index funds or bonds that you have instructed it to buy. This is a set-and-forget system that requires very little time and effort on your part.

The automation should be set up to deposit funds each and every month. As you increase your savings every three months, the deposit and allocations will also increase. Before activating the next tier of the investment account, you would be wise to build up another buffer of three to six months' living expenses in passive investments.

Once you have an extended buffer of liquidity working in passive investments, you may decide to invest in some individual stocks. This is intelligent investing. It's an approach that allows you to have your eggs in all the baskets and maximise your returns.

You have now earned your Tiers of Freedom Investor Badge. You are equipped with knowledge that, if implemented, will put you in the minority of people who reach a level of financial freedom unattainable by the masses.

Individual stock picking

This is where you enter Tier 2. By taking some surplus cash from your automated savings and allocating it to a stock portfolio, you can increase returns and LI via dividends, and boost liquidity. This fits in line with our components for financial freedom.

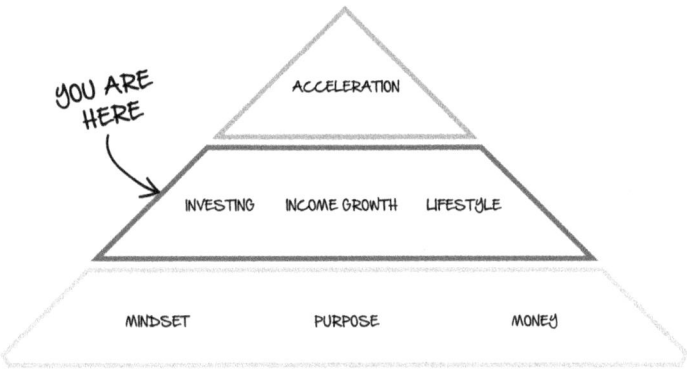

Stock picking is the next step because it allows you to take the next level of risk, and you have earned it because you already have money working for you in the market. You have put your foot in the water, so to speak, and now that you have built up a buffer and gained confidence, your mind is ready to learn new things.

Picking stocks requires a little more time, skill and effort than passive investing. A lack of diversity brings more risk into stock picking, but also brings higher potential rewards.

Within stock picking, there are varying levels of risk as well. Broadly speaking, there are three categories: large cap stocks (the likes of Google, Amazon, Facebook that aren't going anywhere), medium cap stocks (businesses like Peloton that are currently popular, but may have a shorter life) and small cap stocks (startup businesses).

As a rule of thumb, when picking stocks, I look for returns of ideally above 15% to make the process worthwhile. If you can generate 15% returns, you can shorten the run to financial freedom while ensuring you are methodical and sensible in your approach.

The most common way for people to pick stocks is to take advice from peers, colleagues or friends who have absolutely no track record of picking good investments. They hear something on the news or assume that because a certain company is trending in the media, that makes it a good business to invest in. This is wrong. In fact, there are even many business owners who don't understand the basic principles of analysing their own financials, and yet are making decisions to invest in stocks. This is why we are going to start there.

Understanding some basic fundamentals from reading company financials and learning how large organisations and corporations manage their finances can allow you to make better decisions around your own business and personal finances. This can give you a tremendous advantage and edge.

Stocks: What to look for

The first thing you will come across when looking at a stock is what is known as a ticker code.

This is usually a three or four letter code abbreviated from the company name such as AAPL (Apple) or GOOG (Google). Most uninitiated investors look at this code, look at the price per share, then calculate how many shares they can buy, and that's it. They purchase stocks based on no analysis whatsoever other than a feeling or a recommendation from someone.

To understand what a good stock is, you need to be able to read the income statements. Before you do that, there are other terms you must understand in a bit more detail.

Shares outstanding. This is the total amount of shares available or existing in a particular company. If the company has 20,000 shares, then that is the shares outstanding. You can use this information, along with the current share price, to work out the next term.

Market capitalisation (market cap). This is simply the shares outstanding multiplied by the current share price. This is important information because at a glance, you can see how a particular company compares to other large companies. This will also be useful for some simple calculations later on.

Once you understand the shares outstanding and the market cap of the company, it's really about performing some quantitative and qualitative analysis. It starts by understanding the financial statements. Don't worry, this is much easier than you may think.

There are three main financial statements you must understand to perform good analysis of a stock:

- Income statement
- Balance sheet statement
- Cash-flow statement

Looking at one of these statements in isolation will not be enough to perform a quality analysis. Understanding them all will enable you to paint a picture of the company's story, thereby allowing you to make intelligent decisions on your investments. It's difficult for companies to hide poor performance from an investor who can read all three statements. Every public company has these.

Every three months, all public companies are legally required to report their earnings. Earnings season is the point in each quarter when these corporate earnings are released to the public. Historical data is also available on financial sites such as Yahoo! Finance.

Here is a breakdown of each financial statement's purpose.

Income statement. This statement simply displays the revenue income (turnover) and the expenses (outgoings). The bottom figure on this statement is called earnings (net profit).

If a company generates £100,000 in income and has expenses of £80,000, then the earnings would be £20,000. Ideally this figure should be positive. If it's negative, it means the company is not running a profit from its main operations.

Balance sheet statement. This displays the net worth of the company. Just the same as your own personal net worth, it's the sum total of all assets the company owns such as property, plant, machinery etc, with the liabilities to the company, such as loans, deducted. The bottom figure on this statement (which is the assets minus the liabilities) is called the equity in the business.

Cash-flow statement. This tells you exactly how the company is managing the cash in the business. The first line of the cash-flow statement is the operating activity. This is essentially the earnings from the income statement.

This statement also tells you about investment and financing activity. The bottom line of this statement is called net change in cash. This tells you how much cash the company had at the start and the end of the year. A wise metric to look at here is if it is paying down its debts and increasing assets, and how this figure compares to the previous year. Ask yourself:

- Has the profit increased?
- Have the expenses reduced?
- Has the cash increased while the company is paying down debts?
- Has the company purchased more assets?
- Is the company able to generate more profit by spending less or being more efficient with its cash?

Equipped with this information, you can now start to see a story unfold that is transparent enough to aid your investment decisions. However, before you make these decisions, you will need to understand a few more terms and some basic calculations.

Earnings per share (EPS). This is one of the most common figures you will see when looking at financial data. It's simply the earnings on the income statement divided by the shares outstanding. If the company has £20,000 in earnings and 20,000 shares outstanding, the EPS will be £1.

Book value per share (BVPS). This is the equity value on the balance sheet divided by the shares outstanding. If the company has £40,000 of equity, then in this example, we would divide £40,000 by 20,000. In this case, the BVPS would be £2.

Price to earnings ratio (PE). This is simply the price per share divided by the EPS. In this example, if the price per share is £20, then the PE would be £20 divided by £1. In other words, it would be 20.

Price to book ratio (PB). This is the price per share divided by the BVPS. In this example, it would be £20 divided by £2, which would be a PB of 10.

Earnings yield. This is another indication of company value. The calculation is the EPS divided by the price per share multiplied by 100 to give us a percentage. In this example, the EPS is 1, so the earnings yield would be $1 \div 20 \times 100 = 5\%$. This could be used to identify an overvalued stock.

ASSET ACCUMULATION

The way I was taught to think about earnings yield was to imagine a golden goose. Every year, that goose spits out £1,000 worth of golden eggs. The question is, how much would you pay for that goose? If you were to pay £100,000 for it and every year it spat out £1,000 worth of eggs, then your earnings yield would be 1%. If you could somehow buy the same goose for £10,000 and it still spat out £1,000 worth of golden eggs every year, then your earnings yield would be 10%. The earnings yield is basically the PE ratio displayed as a percentage. It's a useful indicator to let you know how much an investment is likely to make you each year based on the amount of cash invested.

Return on equity (ROE). This reflects how well a company is managing the equity in the business. It's simply the earnings divided by the equity multiplied by 100 to get a percentage. In this example, it would be £20,000 divided by £40,000, then multiplied by 100 to get 50%. This figure is extremely important as it shows how efficient a company is at generating profit.

If a company is able to use £40,000 in equity to generate a £20,000 profit, it can indicate that the business is extremely lean and using its cash very wisely to maximise profits. In other words, it does not have to purchase large tangible goods to make a profit. If the ROE is low, then it may indicate that the company is sitting on large amounts of equity and not investing it, or that its operations are not efficient.

Once you understand these terms and how to calculate them, you can start using all of the information to form a story about the company, which will allow you to make better and more informed decisions when investing.

Identifying undervalued stocks

In his book *The Intelligent Investor*,[43] originally published in 1949, financial analyst Benjamin Graham referenced a formula for identifying undervalued stocks using both the PE and PB ratios. Specifically, Graham suggested looking for companies with a PE × PB = <22.5. A low PB ratio provides a high margin of safety and a low PE ratio provides a high earnings yield. Benjamin Graham looked for a PB of less than 1.5 and a PE of less than 15.

As mentioned earlier, none of the methods we've discussed are a complete strategy for picking stocks alone. There are other qualitative and quantitative filters that can be added to your analysis to make an intelligent decision.

How do I question my stock picks?

Whenever I invest in stocks, I run each company through a series of questions to ensure I am making

---

43 B Graham, *The Intelligent Investor: The definitive book on value investing – A book of practical counsel* (Harper & Brothers, 1949)

a well-informed and non-emotional decision. Some questions I might ask are:

- Would I like to own this company for a decade?
- Do I understand the product or service this business is offering?
- Do I use the product or service myself?
- Does the company charge more for its products than its competitors?
- Could any long-term debts be paid off with less than four years' earnings?

Painting a picture of a well-operated company and controlled financial structure will give you great confidence in selecting good stocks to buy. It's much better than taking tips from your middle-class neighbour.

Start building your own watch list of great stocks that tick these boxes and before you know it, you will have confidence in putting your money into well-performing companies.

When to start picking stocks

Let's say you have a pay rise but don't raise your lifestyle costs. Any surplus cash will build up in your savings account until you have enough to pick some stocks. This is where you will use your newfound skills for analysing great stocks.

I like to have a watch list all year round that I score from 0–25, so that when my passive investing account is filled and I have some surplus cash, I have a short-list of stocks that I can take a look at to see if they are a good purchase at the time of my investment. If not, I will continue to wait until the next earnings season.

If I find a good undervalued stock that meets all of my investment criteria, I will take that surplus cash and purchase as many shares of that company as I can. I usually do this every six to twelve months. If after six months there are no promising stocks on my watch list or my watch list stocks all have quite low scores, I will allocate 30% of the surplus cash to my trading account (Tier 3).

The 30% represents my trading to investing ratio. This changes throughout the year depending on my time commitment, my wealth-building agendas and other opportunities. No matter what I allocate to the trading account, I still approach my trading and investing the same way.

Some traders allocate much more to their trading account. Some even put in 100% of their surplus, but I want you to understand that the ones who do that usually trade as a full-time business. Trading isn't something you can dabble in. Unlocking the trading account requires effort, dedication and discipline.

Remember, even if you just do the Tier 3 investing, you can build enormous wealth over a long period of time by having that tier set up and automated. It all depends on your appetite for risk and what your motive is.

Why invest in companies and not property or something else?

There have been countless times in the past when I have been asked why I choose not to invest in property. Although I know plenty of property investors who have managed to do very well, it is important to put your money into assets that align with your personality and agenda.

When I speak to the successful property investors, they have spent years managing deals, project managing, getting their hands dirty, dealing with bad tenants, paying out for costly repairs and maintenance fees, and yet they still have a love for the game. They are ambitious in property and they embrace the rough with the smooth.

Investing in property can be extremely rewarding if managed correctly and liberating with the right investment structure, but there is a huge difference between masterfully managing a property investment portfolio with the objective of financial freedom and buying a house to live in, which is what most people think will make them financially free. This is why I am cagey when it comes to talking about property investments. Most people simply can't see the difference between an investment and ploughing their money into a product of the bank.

I also see many people becoming too attached to property investments, which causes them to make poor decisions. The moment you become emotional over any investment, you have already lost.

With that aside, the main reason I prefer to invest in companies as opposed to property is because I have always thought it wise to invest in assets that are growing in value in line with evolution and without me, instead of an asset that is deteriorating constantly and reliant on me to keep repairing it and patching it up. Evolution is a move towards maximum simplicity. Every earnings season, one of the main performance indicators of a company is how much profit it is able to generate without the expenditure of property, plant, equipment and physical goods that suffer wear and tear or have a requirement for overhead maintenance.

In a single year, a car manufacturer might turn over £100 billion and report a profit of £1 billion. Although the profit of £1 billion looks impressive, to generate that profit, they have had to spend £99 billion, a large portion of which will be on property, plant, equipment and materials. In other words, tangible goods that are subject to wear and tear. These companies require maximum output for minimum input due to the nature of the business.

On the other hand, a software company might turn over £100 billion and report profits of £40 billion. When you look at the expenditure of the company on the cash flow statement, you will find it is able to generate a much higher profit without spending so much on property, plant, equipment and materials.

The most profitable companies in the world are able to make the highest profits by buying into less complex entropic systems. Entropy is a process of breaking down, introducing complexities, chaos, deterioration and decay. As soon as you purchase a physical thing, it starts deteriorating. A brick, a piece of equipment or plant will break down and dissolve over time. As soon as it's put together, it starts eroding and decaying, and you have entropy going against you.

However, the great minds behind the business that designed that particular material or piece of equipment continue to innovate and create even better and more sustainable versions of it. If you invest in the company rather than the equipment, you essentially put your money into some of the brightest entrepreneurs dedicated to solving problems and making products that are more efficient, more sustainable and providing real value to the world. As soon as they have launched Mark 1, they are working on Mark 2.

With business, you have an element of life and innovation. With plant, property and materials, you've got decay and erosion. Whatever building goes up has to come down at some point. As a species, we humans are destroying and rebuilding property all the time. Commercial properties in London are completely refurbished once every twenty-five years on average.[44] That doesn't include all of the smaller tenant refurbishments that take place every two to three years internally. Buildings are always in a cycle of repair. The best businesses, however, are in perpetual innovation and growth.

Just to give you an example, as part of one of the index funds that I hold, I own a tiny piece of Microsoft. When a competitor to Microsoft decides to try and compete with it on a certain product, be it a new piece of software, a video game console or an operating system, some of the best minds on the planet arrange a meeting around a boardroom table while I am sitting at home or asleep, and ask the question, 'How can we improve our product and become better?' They are collectively figuring out how Microsoft can serve a larger number of people and change lives to a greater degree, and do it for a competitive or even a cheaper cost.

While I am asleep, the sliver of that company that I own is forever growing in line with innovation and

---

44   D Albrice, 'How Long Do Buildings Last?', RDH Blog (28 January 2015), www.rdh.com/blog/long-buildings-last, accessed 15 April 2025

human evolution as opposed to having the decaying effect going against it.

Property is a time capsule

My house was built in 1910 and, like many houses, was constructed from a variety of different products and materials such as bricks, mortar, tiles, PVC, lead, timber etc.

The minds behind the businesses that designed those materials were innovators. They were no doubt trying to pioneer different ways to come up with more sustainable PVC that wouldn't lose colour in the sun, better types of tiles that could stand harsher weather conditions and stronger timber. When they released their product, at that particular moment in time, it was the best it could be. However, as soon as the house was built, the innovation was frozen in time and from that point on, everything started decaying.

What I am reiterating here is that when you buy into a property, you've got entropy going against you. When you are investing in companies and minds, you are investing in the directional flow of natural evolution. The financial chart of the S&P 500 represents historical human evolution on planet Earth.

Often when people invest in property, they make the mistake of thinking they're going to get a ROI after living there for a few years. What they don't take into consideration are the maintenance and repair costs, the grass growing, the fences falling down, the driveway sagging, the roof growing moss, the gutters clogging up and all of the service charges and fuel bills that come with it. If they factored that into the investment, they would realise that they hadn't actually made much money at all.

To summarise, I am not against property investment, but I prefer to invest my money into evolution. I have found that it's more efficient and aligned with my values of freedom.

Congratulations on earning your Baller Badge! You are now accelerating your way to financial freedom.

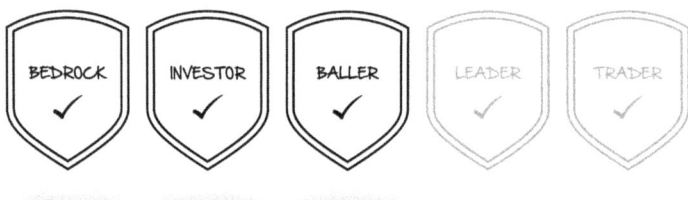

TOP TIP

Trading isn't speculation and speculation isn't trading. I can't stress this enough! You need specific strategies for passive investing, you need different strategies for trading and different strategies again for speculating. Do not make the mistake of trying to apply passive investment strategies to trading, they will not work.

14
Leveraged Income

When you get to the stage where you are able to automate your investments and have a structured tiered investment account speeding up returns on your money, you are starting to generate LI into this system to accelerate your journey to financial freedom. The next job is to create more LI streams (mobile and passive) to pump as much money (liquidity) into the system as possible. The more you create, the faster you will reach your financial goals.

The key here is to raise income, but to do it in the right way, one that doesn't sacrifice your time and freedom. Focusing on types of income and having an understanding of how to shift from active to mobile to passive income streams, and then build multiple systems that allow you to replicate the process, is what will liberate you from doing uninspiring work and push you into a constant flow of LI. By doing so, you will be more vibrant, have more energy and life force, and as a result, naturally earn more money than ever.

There are people who earn millions of pounds per year and people who earn minimum wage. More often than not, both of these groups will have relative prosperity. In other words, if the people in either of them lost their income today, they would have fewer than thirty days to live before radically having to change their lifestyle.

High income earners are no better off than low income earners if their strategies are wrong. Income can be one of the most important elements to building wealth, if it's built the right way, but the key is in the types of income that are developed and how you use them to become financially free. If you develop the wrong types of income that aren't aligned with financial freedom, you will never feel free.

Remember, you certainly do not want to trade time for money because your time is priceless. Also remember never to limit the amount of income streams available to you. The average millionaire has seven solid income streams.[45] It's wise to continually grow yours.

---

45 K Vandenboss, 'The average millionaire has 7 sources of income: Here are 3 you can start building today' (Yahoo! Finance, 30 May 2024), https://finance.yahoo.com/news/average-millionaire-7-sources-income-164311915.html, accessed 21 October 2024

Income growth

Although having a high income is not directly correlated to being financially free, growing your income and managing it well can definitely accelerate the process. It's wise to consider ways to raise your income, but in a way that does not jeopardise your freedom.

With time and freedom being the objectives, the goal is to develop the most efficient streams possible that allow you to scale your income to ever-growing degrees without attaching your time to it. In other words, you want to do something you love, but generate income by being less active, more mobile and more passive. The more mobile you are, the freer you feel. The more passive the income source is, the freer you feel.

This type of LI only comes from assets that you either buy or create. The order here is important, though. Many people struggle chasing passive income and never obtain it. This is because they have neglected the steps to get them there. Mobile first, then passive.

People often tell me they want passive income. When I ask them what that looks like, they reply with something like, 'I just want to be able to work from a beach somewhere.' As I stressed earlier, this is not passive income; this is mobile income.

Most of the time, people are actually trying to achieve mobile income. Once income becomes mobile, we can then focus on automations, systems, delegations and processes that reduce the amount of time required from us to generate that income.

Imagine your life like a game of Tetris. The first shape drops down and it's a bit clunky and inefficient. Your job is to make it as compact (spaceless) as possible, which in turn frees up more time. If you can make your active workload as spaceless – in other words, mobile – as possible, you are halfway to freedom.

You may be surprised at how free you will feel when you can do your job from anywhere.

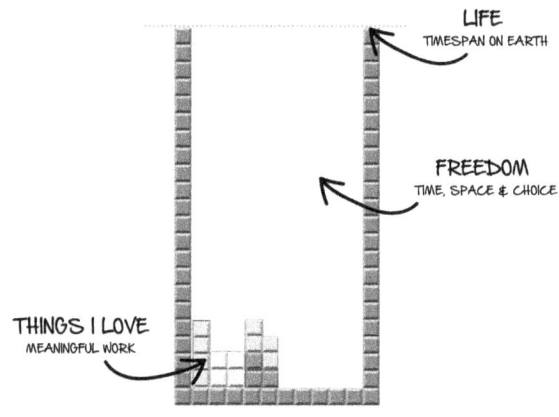

Life is like a game of Tetris

Income is something that should flow to you naturally as a result of the love and creativity you put into the world, and then be fed into an ordered system of satisfying the senses, developing and growing wealth as efficiently as possible. This process should be automatic and emotionless while keeping you free and creative to get on with your mission.

The only way to achieve pure passive income is by having your wealth invested and managed for you. This is the ultimate goal. Until then, you must understand the income types.

Types of income

The only way to get more income is from other human beings. There are two ways of achieving this:

- Better them at a skill such as boxing, poker, trading etc. This is known as a zero-sum income method.
- Serve them with services, products etc. This is known as a positive-sum income method (a concept I'll be exploring in my next book that focuses on building products and starting a business).

My advice is to do both.

I have found few people who generate income from a pure zero-sum business. They may start out with this kind of business, but after a while, they lack fulfilment and find a desire to serve. For this reason, it's wise to master both. Service is the greatest gift to humanity and allows you to get what you want while helping others get what they want. I believe that we all get what we want in life to the degree we help others do the same.

There are several ways to serve people, but the type of income each one generates will determine your level of freedom, fulfilment and reward. Some examples are:

- One-to-one consulting: inefficient, limited profitability, active.
- Coach: one-to-many, active, mobile.
- Website designer: mobile, non-passive, limited income.
- High-street shop owner: non-mobile, non-passive, inefficient, set hours, limited profitability.
- YouTube vlogger: active, mobile, non-passive.
- Online freelancer: mobile, active, limited capacity.
- Online digital marketer: mobile, active, although semi-passive if structured correctly.

As you will see from the list, all these examples require an active role to be played by the business owner most of the time. However, all of these businesses have the capability to bolt on a passive income model. How?

- Create a digitally delivered product that is automatically distributed to the world 24/7.
- Segregate business income and invest in innovation, systems, teams, automations.
- Segregate personal income from the business to pay into passive investments, stocks and speculation.

When structured the right way, these strategies allow you not only to travel the world and be flexible, but also to build more passive income than active income, which means you do not have to work hard to cover your cost of living. The more time you have, the more money you earn naturally as a by-product.

Ways to improve your income

Have time as the objective in mind. Ask yourself how you can take what you do now and make part/all of it mobile first, then passive. When you're thinking about this, also consider how you can serve people more efficiently.

Here are some ideas of how to enhance your income:

- **Have a bigger impact on people's lives**. Measure how much of a difference you are making in your clients' lives and continuously work on improving that score. Provide more value than anyone else you know and *never* reduce your price.

- **Reach more people**. We live in a world where you have the power to pick up your phone and speak to millions of people at once. Service doesn't always have to be in the form of a product. Your words, values and message can be used to build a strong following who resonate with you. Building a product or service as a next step will allow your business to become global.

- **Serve higher-income earners.** Even if you can make a 10% difference to someone's life, the amount they will pay for your service will be relative to their own income. If you work on serving higher-income earners, then you can charge more for your products and services and they will happily pay.

- **Serve people more frequently.** If you have one product, build two. Consider what the next logical step is for your customers to make them clients. What market can you explore? What product can you develop? What territory can you enter? Who can you partner with to make this happen?

- **Stop working.** If you are unhappy in your job or business, instead of thinking about working more or harder, see how you can climb your way out of it while you build a side hustle or skill that does inspire and excite you. Don't wait until you have a bit more money because you will be chasing that forever. Instead, believe in yourself, get educated and go for it. You will earn more doing something you are motivated to do from within than you will doing something that requires you to find motivation externally.

From now on, instead of thinking about small incremental income growth, ask yourself, 'What can I do to double my income?' Find out all the sources of

LEVERAGED INCOME

your income or everything you do in your job and ask yourself, 'How can I provide that in half the time and more efficiently and to more people?'

Author of *Secrets of the Millionaire Mind* Harv Eker says: 'It's not so much a "what" you do, but rather a "how" you do it. Leverage uses specific tactics and strategies that allow you to work smarter instead of harder.'[46] Leverage in business income starts with replacing yourself or much of what you do personally. Constantly ask yourself, 'How can I provide people with value in the form of my products and services while I sleep?' If you are looking at starting a business, re-launching your business or working for someone else, I recommend you create products and services structured in such a way that they are passive, mobile, scaleable and profitable.

I have found that the sweet-spot model for this is to have 80% of your revenue coming from a digital access product (like Netflix) and the other 20% coming from an ongoing digital product which keeps the business feeling new and exciting and ultimately extends the life-time customer value of your clients. This is one of the most important metrics in business. Structuring your business model this way allows you to be rewarded, fulfilled and free all at the same time as maintaining fair exchange with your clients.

---

[46] TH Eker, *Secrets of the Millionaire Mind: Mastering the inner game of wealth* (Harper Business, 2005)

To hear me speak more about this, go to www.alwaysfree.com/businessincome.

Once you have examined your income streams and found ways to generate LI, you are getting much closer to financial freedom. You may decide that Tier 3 and Tier 2 investing is enough to support you and your desired lifestyle at this point, but if you want to take the next step, it is time to look at what trading (Tier 1) can offer. First, though, you have to earn your right to unlock this final step on the pyramid.

You are now a Leader. You can do what you love and be rewarded at the same time as accelerating your financial freedom journey even more.

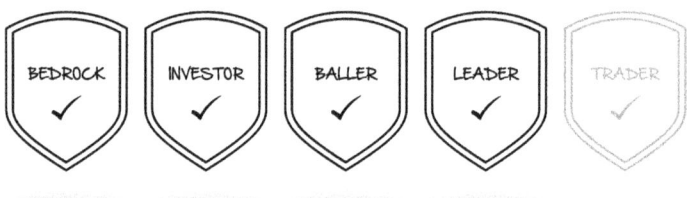

TOP TIP

How wealthy and prosperous you become relies little on income if you are not focused on how that can serve your purpose. Earning more can make you richer and enhance your lifestyle, but 99% of the time you'll end up stressed, working harder and longer, with more problems and challenges than you can deal with. This is because of the types of income you are focusing on.

15
Trading

Trading is a skill that takes a considerable amount of time to learn and master. I recommend you unlock the trading account only once you are comfortable that you have learned to trade consistently profitably and have a tested, verified and repeatable system that has proven results from a demonstration account.

In my experience, and backed up in a number of studies, trading and speculation is around 20% technical and 80% mental.[47] Before you attempt to use capital for speculation, it is essential that you are comfortable

---

47 BJ Bloch, 'How to develop a "trading brain"' (Investopedia, 21 December 2023), www.investopedia.com/articles/basics/13/how-to-develop-trading-brain.asp, accessed 16 April 2025 and C. Thompson, 'Trading psychology: What it is and importance' (Investopedia, 26 June 2023), www.investopedia.com/articles/trading/02/110502.asp, accessed 16 April 2025

with technical analysis, risk management, brokers' orders, spreads, overnight rolling costs etc. Most of my profitable clients need around eighteen months before trading live, which is when they have realistic expectations of their system and a solid plan for consistent profits with minimal drawdowns.

Trading has allowed me to take a portion of my investment account and accelerate returns to the degree of 36% on average. Even though my first year's trading netted me 76%, my second year netted 27% followed by 32% in year three, but it has eventually averaged out over time at around 36%.

Having a long-term mean view on your results will help you stay grounded and conservative when it comes to profit taking. Personally, for trading to be worth learning and become a profession for me, I needed returns of over 25%. Any lower and my time and capital may have been better put to use in other speculations or business. Because most of my trading is semi-passive (fifteen minutes per day), I am happy with a 36% average return per year. Who wouldn't be?

Trading for me was the final piece in the wealth acceleration puzzle. Per annum, I am returning 10% on passive investments, 15% on my stocks and 36% on my trading account. The cumulative returns are around 20% across my entire investment portfolio, which allowed me to replace my income in three and a half years.

Now you have a sustainable model for building wealth, the next step is to accelerate it further. However, this step is optional and situation specific. I consider savings as compulsory, passive investing as a necessity, stock picking as optional and trading as not for everyone, even though it's one of the most accessible wealth accelerating vehicles I know of.

You will know if trading is for you or not. If you reach a threshold of liquidity of twelve months' LEs working for you in the markets and still decide you want to learn to trade, remember what I said about your mindset in terms of removing emotions from the process. Once you have built the system the right way, ie with automations doing the heavy lifting, you have a higher chance of succeeding.

If you're considering trying your hand at trading and speculation, then what I'm about to share with you is essential. Studies consistently show that the vast majority of new traders lose money early on—often within the first few months.[48] In fact, research suggests that over 70% of retail traders end up losing capital, primarily due to lack of preparation, poor risk management and emotional decision-making.[49] By understanding what really drives success in trading,

---

48 A Farley, 'The casino mentality in trading' (Investopedia, 2 November 2023), www.investopedia.com/articles/investing/070815/casino-mentality-trading.asp, accessed 15 April 2025
49 O Groette, 'Day Trading statistics 2025: The hard truth' (Quantified Strategies, 31 December 2024), www.quantifiedstrategies.com/day-trading-statistics, accessed 15 April 2025

you'll put yourself in the small minority who actually have a chance of making it work to your advantage.

There are many types of speculation such as flipping property, stocks, art, fine wine, classic cars, jewellery. As I have been able to achieve a good level of success in trading the foreign currency markets, this will be my focus for this chapter. I have split the rest of the chapter into two parts to help you digest and assimilate all of the information it shares.

Part I – Why trading?

When I was at a stage where I was projecting forward ten years before I could replace my income, I became very frustrated with the position I was in. I was paying myself as much as I could so the business had little cash flow to employ the staff and talent it needed. I had little interest in the industry and had completely lost enthusiasm for the operations. At that point, it was time to accelerate things. I was determined to get my financial independence time frame down even further.

That's when I looked at speculation.

At first, I explored online poker, options trading and various other highly speculative vehicles for accelerating my wealth. I knew that if I took a small allocation of my investment account, around 20–30%, and I could master trading, I would be able to significantly reduce my run to financial independence.

In the pursuit of mastering consistent profits (which seemed like smoke and mirrors at one point), I dedicated almost three years and donated over £40,000 to 'learning' the markets. I took two-day courses, followed online 'gurus' and used automated trading systems.

The good news is that during this time, I learned a hell of a lot about what didn't work, and what did. Once I became consistently profitable towards the end of the third year, I conservatively predicted that if I was able to keep on averaging the results I was getting at the time, I would be able to replace the income I needed for my lifestyle completely within five years.

My plan was to average around 20% returns per annum based on a mixed portfolio of my passive investments, commodities, REITs, stocks and bonds returning around 10–15% per year, and my trading returns of 30–35% per year. Between the two, I could average out the returns at 20% while allowing for some wiggle room. This meant I could be financially independent within five years.

I underestimated. I ended up completely replacing my income and more within three and a half years.

Simple? Yes, it can be, but easy? Far from it.

Is it easy once you know how? No.

As I said, trading and speculation requires far more skill than anything else we have covered in this book. What I am about to share with you will open your eyes to some of the mistakes I made and give you insights to help set your expectations. Then, should you wish to participate in trading and speculation, you will be far better equipped technically and, more importantly, mentally.

If played right, trading can be extremely rewarding, but I hope you can see the importance of implementing the earlier stages of this book first. It's essential that you have the right mindset and long time horizons with trading if you are to learn, master and profit consistently.

The key word here is 'consistently'.

Anyone can win a lucky bet, but have you tried feeding your family by doing so? If you think learning to trade is stressful, try buying your weekly groceries using your returns from it with no other income stream.

Seriously, I want you to keep consistency in your mind as we go through this chapter. If you do, you will fully appreciate why trading and speculation is the final tier of my investment account.

I have lost track of the number of times people have told me they want to be consistently profitable only to go and change their approach as soon as they perceive things to be going sideways. To be consistently profitable, you must start with and base your entire trading approach on consistency.

The wealth accelerator

The framework I am going to share with you is one I wholeheartedly believe in after blowing tens of thousands of pounds and spending almost 20,000 hours in the markets at the time of writing this book.

As I mentioned before, it's common to start wanting to trade and speculate to get greater returns on your investments. Speculation can yield extraordinarily high returns. During my first year trading professionally, I returned 76% in eleven months. Trading the financial markets is what allowed me to accelerate my returns enough to replace my job income in under four years.

The reason 90% of traders fail to become consistently profitable is because they use the wrong approach. Due to the way trading is flaunted by flaky con artists on the internet, coupled with the fact that most human beings want to chase pleasure and avoid pain, they usually end up skipping the fundamental foundational work and jump straight to the strategies.

Assuming that trading is at least 80% psychological and 20% technical, if you master the approach, the act becomes easy. The question is, if you could spend two years developing a skill that would allow you to accelerate your wealth to the degree of 25+% per year, would you take the chance? Considering the banks are offering 0.2% interest per year at the time of writing, I don't know many people who would not find that an attractive option.

Process over outcome thinking is crucial if you are to have any hope of generating consistent returns. Being focused entirely on the outcome can lead you to pass by opportunities along the way and not recognise where your approach might be costing you. Trust that the process will lead you to the outcome you desire, be consistent about applying what works and enjoy the journey.

Trading has allowed me to understand people better, manage greater degrees of risk, be more self-aware and objective, focus on longer-term outcomes and so much more. I have had the experience of earning four and a half times the average person's annual salary in six hours. I have sat at a bar in a beach bungalow in the middle of the Indian Ocean while covering the cost of the entire trip with a few clicks of my mouse. There are many extraordinary benefits to trading, but unless you go into it with the right mindset and realistic expectations, you have a very slim chance of succeeding.

If you want to master such a powerful skill, give yourself time. This is not something you will learn in two days, a week or even a month. Give yourself a year to learn and a year to start generating consistent profits. It may take a little less time and it may take a little longer; either way, it will be worth it.

It's all down to your approach

One question I hear consistently is, 'Isn't trading just large-scale gambling?' When I started to learn how to trade the financial markets, many people thought I was turning to gambling and as a result, I endured some stress in my relationships. Even those who were close to me questioned my actions. For this reason, many people become extremely wary about participating in any form of trading.

Another reason people are wary is lack of education on risk management. Of everything you will discover in this book, trading and speculation requires the most skill, the most time to learn, the most mental effort, the highest level of potential risk, and therefore brings the highest level of potential reward. This is why I advise you only to consider trading once you have built up Tier 3 and Tier 2 of your investing account structure.

Most retail traders end up giving all of their money back to the minority who manage their risk wisely. When I get asked if trading is risky, my answer is always yes, but the risk has nothing to do with the market. The market is just the market. It does what it does every single day with or without your involvement. It doesn't care if you participate or not and it certainly is not responsible for how you manage your risk.

Las Vegas casinos are open all year round. Each and every day, thousands of people try their hand at winning money. The reason the casinos are so profitable is because the croupiers understand that the majority of their punters are approaching them for a bit of fun. There is no consistency, no game plan and no edge.

If you have ever been to a casino and had a lucky win, you will have been encouraged to keep playing by the croupier because they know that if you play long enough without consistency or an edge, you will end up giving back most or all of the money you've won to the casino. The casino always wins.

However, have you ever noticed that it's the same faces around the winning poker tournament table? They are there every night. They consistently reach the semi-final and final rounds of the tournaments. In fact, most of these players fund their lifestyle from their profits. Why is this? Why is it that some people are able to generate consistent profits from gambling, or trading, while most people end up losing?

The differentiator between the participant who consistently generates a positive return and the participant who consistently loses money has nothing to do with the casino or the market. It has everything to do with a decision. A decision whether to approach the process as a gambler or a professional business owner.

How you approach speculation will dictate whether you earn money from it long term. If you are approaching it as a professional, you will be poised, strategic, systematic, and have a solid plan for managing risk at all times. You will have routine procedures and contingencies in place to ensure your actions are never by chance. As you earn your right to greater degrees of risk, you treat your investment capital with more respect.

One last thing to mention here is that there will always be a lag between what you say you are going to achieve and the actual results. This can be frustrating when it comes to trading and cause doubt in people around you.

There are some unrealistic expectations towards trading and what is achievable in twelve months. When people realise it's more difficult than they anticipated, they can become discouraged and, as a result, underestimate what is achievable in the following twenty-four months. However, get it right and this is where the magic happens.

It can be hard to stay focused when everyone around you is doubting your ability. You have shared your vision with them, and all they see is someone spending a lot of time trying to master something they think you should be succeeding at by now.

This is why trading can be a lonely pursuit. Let your results do the talking.

Become a trading system developer

An edge in trading is gained through having a profitable system developed via high-quality setups, a trade plan, a method for carrying out pre-market analysis, a money management strategy, a risk management strategy, a trading journal, a method for optimisation and the discipline to execute everything consistently.

Like any discipline, an edge is ever evolving. Trading is no different. People who are successful at trading the financial markets year after year are continuously developing and optimising their trading plan to greater degrees of efficiency, effectiveness and profitability.

Every trading system has winning streaks and losing streaks. It is common for people to be attracted to a system that is going through a winning streak. They try to trade it themselves until it hits a natural losing streak, and then they chase the next winning system. Looking for an ever-profitable system is like relying on someone to give you water instead of digging a well. Because there are so many components to a successful trading system, it's far wiser to understand how to build your own.

Two people can have wildly different approaches. One of them will be able to trade the market and make money consistently. The other will lose money. Why is this?

The person trading the market profitably has developed a strategy.

Every successful trader I have met has embraced personalised system development. This means they have learned the principles of trading, then built a system to suit their personal situational requirements. I am going to share with you some advice on what to pay attention to when developing your system.

Courses do not work

Whether you put it to the side and never bothered to start it or you just didn't get the outcome you thought you would from it, there are many reasons why trying to learn to trade by taking a course will stop you getting results. If you are watching a pre-recorded course in an online portal, what makes you think you are going to log in and actually go through the information in the right order? No one is watching you. No one is there to hold your hand or guide you through from start to finish. If you are not internally motivated to get through the course, you won't.

Nuances

Have you ever watched a film a second time and noticed things that you didn't see the first time? This is because your mind is constantly generalising information and filling in gaps based on your previous experiences, beliefs and perceptions. If the information you are taking in doesn't quite fit those experiences, beliefs and perceptions, sometimes the brain will distort it to make it fit.

This is a mechanism to make us more efficient, but it can have a detrimental effect on our ability to retain crucial information in certain situations, learning to trade being one of them. We might ignore information that our brain decides isn't important when in actual fact it can be the difference between succeeding or spending another year learning.

Any apprentice can go to college and learn theory. It's not until the apprentice goes out on site in the real world that they truly learn about fault finding, objection handling, problems and emergencies. When they are in a live environment, they learn more about the skill and the application in one month than they did in two years at college.

Trading is the same. Having a mentor in the real markets to show you the day-to-day nuances is what will separate you from the other apprentices.

When you're considering learning to trade, I recommend looking for an educator who provides all of these:

- **Mentorship**: Coaching and guidance through the market nuances.

- **Live trading environment**. Being able to watch them trade live will give you belief transference and confidence.

- **Tools**. Having access to trading business tools will allow you to become a successful system developer.

- **Community or teams**. Being around like-minded traders with the same goal will keep you disciplined and force you into objectivity.

- **Dedicated question time**. Everyone has a different attention span. Make sure you can access your mentors at regular intervals to go through answers to your questions in detail.

- **Course material**. Yes, you will actually need high-quality learning material. The material should include basic terminology, position sizing calculations, information on brokers, risk management, money management and how to develop a trading business.

For a good, well-rounded foundation, I recommend you check out the Tier One Trading Emergence programme, which is free. Go to www.tiersoffreedom.com/tierone.

Don't learn everything

It's common for people to consume vast amounts of information on trading and use resource sites that are essentially encyclopaedias. They think that the more they know about trading, the better a trader they will be.

This isn't true.

The more you learn about different styles of trading, indicators and strategies, the more you will be susceptible to forming conflicting biases and analyses in the market. One bias will be telling you to buy and the other telling you to sell. This conflict will paralyse you from being able to execute trades.

To move forward in your trading efficiently and effectively, you must understand enough about enough to allow you to place a well-calculated trade. That starts with understanding your appetite for risk.

Part II – Risk appetite

Everyone has a different appetite for risk, which is why, although there are a lot of hidden personal benefits to learning to trade, it's certainly not for everyone.

Due to the level of risk you can be exposed to in volatile speculative markets, it's often perceived that trading has to be extremely risky. This is not true. You can build a trading system that is wildly profitable while managing risk to suit your appetite. It's all about position sizing and protecting your capital.

Risking too much of your capital on each trade will make it difficult for you to get back to breakeven. In fact, if you lose 50% of your trading capital, you then have to make 100% back again just to break even. The shortest time in which I have doubled my trading capital is eighteen months, and that was without withdrawals.

I have found that people who are unfulfilled or have unresolved pains, blames and resentments usually have a tendency to chase a quick fix. These people have a high appetite for risk for the wrong reasons. This is why I waited until this section of the book to even mention this level of risk.

Then there are those who are irrationally risk averse. The fact you are reading this book suggests to me that you are not one of those people. You understand that irrational risk aversion will guarantee mediocrity in life. To have an extraordinary life, you must take calculated risks.

The key is to understand where you sit on the personality scale.

Assessing your personality

People who succeed at trading understand that they need to match their trading system to suit their personality. Speculation requires maximum testing of your comfort zone. Trying to force something that isn't suited to your personality is a recipe for disaster.

When it comes to designing a trading routine, it pays to consider a few things in respect of matching it to your personality.

Strike rate

How often are you right? Some traders like to be right more than they are wrong, some traders are happy to be wrong more than they are right as long as they get the reward to risk profile they need to remain calm in a drawdown.

Reward to risk profile

This is the amount of risk on the table on any one trade correlated to the potential reward.

Depending on the strike rate of the system or the style of trading, some traders like to have a 1:1 reward to risk profile, some prefer to have a 3:1 profile or more. In most cases, the lower the strike rate, the higher the reward to risk.

Opportunity

Some traders like to have lots of opportunities to feel they are active. Some traders are happy with fewer opportunities, knowing their system is highly profitable. Remember, there is no time-for-money correlation with trading. How much time you spend at your computer is purely a personally driven choice.

If you have been used to exchanging time for money all your working life, it can be uncomfortable when you first start trading and find few opportunities. This can result in over trading or forcing trades. For this reason, it is wise to develop a system that provides more opportunities in the beginning so that you aren't at risk of jeopardising your results. Later on, once you have controlled and balanced your emotions a little better (and maybe taken up a hobby), you can tweak the system to produce fewer opportunities.

The diagram below shows the approximate averages when it comes to the relationship between strike rate and reward to risk.

REWARD	RISK	WIN RATE
0.1	1	91%
0.2	1	83%
0.5	1	67%
1	1	50%
2	1	33%
3	1	25%
5	1	17%
10	1	9%
20	1	5%

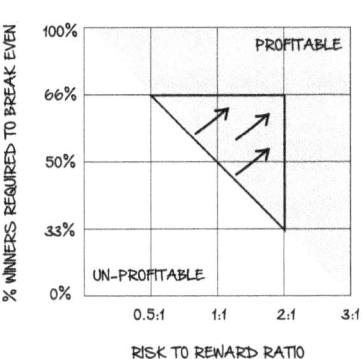

The middle section indicated with arrows is where most traders find their sweet spots.

Most traders I work with settle for a 50%–55% strike rate, but I know a few institutional traders who are happy to be wrong seven times out of ten because they have an 8:1 reward to risk profile.

Positive expectancy

The most important thing is that your system has a positive expectancy. How much do you win when you are right? How much do you lose when you are wrong? How often are you right?

Most traders settle for 50%.

Your lifestyle

Your lifestyle will also affect your style of and approach to trading. The key to being a consistently profitable trader is having the ability to execute a consistent plan. If you are trying to force trading into your life at times that are inconvenient, then your lack of consistency will mean you suffer. You must not 'dabble' in trading.

I suggest making it easy to be consistent. Set yourself up for success and make it difficult to fail. Start by considering what time of the day is best for you to consistently dedicate to chart time (a trading chart is a visual that shows the price movement of an asset over a period of time). Even in a learning phase, it pays to build a habit of consistency. Setting a consistent time and routine forms an anchor for learning and trading professionally.

Time frames

The great thing about trading is that you can build a plan to suit your daily routine. You have access to charts on multiple time frames, which means you can decide whether to check them once, four times, eight times or more per day.

Swing trading is a style where you are trading longer-term moves in the market. It typically requires less screen time simply due to the management of opportunities. Day trading is referred to as higher-frequency trading, normally on a lower time frame like the fifteen-minute or five-minute charts. This requires more focus, more screen time and is a much noisier environment.

I don't recommend anyone starts day trading until they have mastered consistency and profits in the higher time frame system of swing trading.

As consistency is the most important thing, when you're choosing a time frame to trade on, I have a few rules of thumb:

- If you can check the charts one to two times per day, consider trading the daily time frames only.

- If you can check the charts three to four times per day, consider trading the four-hour time frames.

- If you can check more than four times per day, then consider the sixty-minute or lower time frames.

I recommend that all beginners start on the higher time frames and only consider lower time frames when they have developed their skills. Once these skills are developed, they can be used the same way across all time frames.

Style of trading

There are many ways to make money trading the markets, but the markets themselves are only ever in three different phases:

- When a market is going up, it is called a bullish trend.

- When a market is going down, it is called a bearish trend.

- When a market is going sideways, this is referred to as a range or consolidation zone.

You can make money trading a bullish trend, a bearish trend and in consolidation zones. You can trade in the direction of the trend and make money. You can trade against the trend and make money. As long as your strategy is consistent, you will have one of only three outcomes:

- You will make money over time.
- You will lose money over time.
- You will break even over time.

Your job as a trader is to build a consistently profitable system just like any other business.

Trading is a business

Trading is a business in terms of supply and demand, income and expenses, and duplication of a system to make consistent profits. If you are to run a successful trading business, you must treat it like one.

A trading business is no riskier than any other business. According to the Office for National Statistics, the five-year survival rate for UK businesses born in 2018 is 39.4%, indicating that approximately 60.6% of businesses fail within their first five years.[50] Furthermore, as of the start of 2024, only 26% of UK private sector businesses had employees, and about 4.8% had more than ten employees.

---

50 ONS, 'Business demography, UK: 2023' (Statistical Bulletin, 18 November 2024), www.ons.gov.uk/businessindustryandtrade/business/activitysizeandlocation/bulletins/businessdemography/2023/pdf, accessed 15 April 2025

Trading requires no employees, no complex tax rules, no shop front, no physical product and no customers. The fact that most people fail at trading only indicates that they are not treating it like a business.

Successful trading is a game of probability, not certainty, so it is important to realise that all trading strategies will have losses. Losing trades is simply a cost of doing business. In a 'normal' business, you might have costs such as rent, salespeople, vehicles, production and other overheads. You need to pay these costs to produce your product or service. When you sell a product or service, the costs have all been built into the price and there will be a profit margin.

There are always costs you pay to do business. The difference between other business and trading is that every time you make a sale, you know on a unit-by-unit basis what your profit and loss will look like.

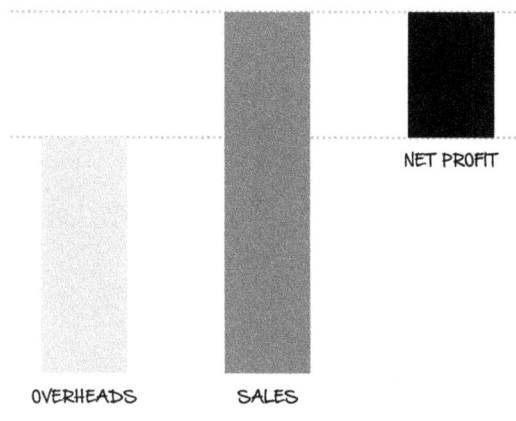

Regular business

In trading, you might have a week of winning trades, then a week of losing trades. You might go for one month at breakeven, then have a few highly profitable days. You never know what opportunities the markets are going to present you with, so the profit and loss does not come in a unit-by-unit fashion. Instead, at the end of the month, you will have winning trades (income), you will have losing trades, broker fees, data feeds, software etc (costs of doing business), and lastly, you will have the difference between the two which is, of course, your profit.

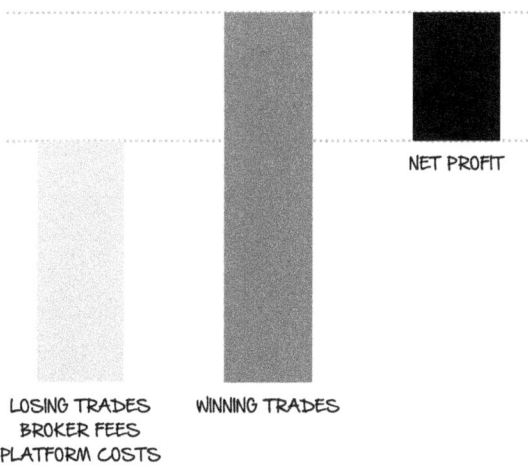

Trading business

For this reason, it is extremely important to have longer time horizons that allow you to focus on performance over time instead of a sale-by-sale basis.

Markets are your employees

Markets have different personalities. They all perform differently. Some are stronger in certain strategies than others. Some work well together, and they all like to take a holiday from time to time. There are certain periods of time where nothing will happen.

Having a perspective like this will help you to remain focused on managing your portfolio professionally.

Imagine starting a business and employing twenty people on day one. You would not be able to manage them. You wouldn't see who were the leaders, who was losing you money, who had strengths in certain departments and who worked well together. You would not be able to organise them all in an effective way to maximise profit.

Instead, you might employ two or three and manage them until they could be macromanaged. You would then employ a fourth and fifth, managing them until they could be macromanaged, and so on.

It surprises me how often traders start off expecting to manage ten or more currency pairs from day one. It's a recipe for disaster. Remember, consistency is key. It's difficult to stay consistent with too much going on to handle. Start small and work your way up the management ladder.

Trading is a book in itself, which is why I wrote one called *Trading Free*. I won't go over the technicals here. Instead, I recommend you pick up a copy if you are interested in unlocking Tier 1 of your investment account and accelerating your returns.

If you want to learn to trade, the benefits can be extraordinary. Apart from being one of the greatest self-discovery processes I have ever been through, trading can generate income that can be classed as semi-passive and highly leveraged, so it fits well within the components of financial freedom.

TOP TIP

It's a common misconception that to be a good trader, you must be a mathematical wizard or have a degree in economics. If you understand logic and how to build assets in your trading business, you can become a fantastic trader. If this is something you would like to learn about in more detail, you can go to www.alwaysfree.com/tradingfree where you can also grab a copy of my book *Trading Free*.

16
Hedging

Hedging is a term used commonly in investing for diversifying and minimising risk in the case of an asset dropping in value. A simple way to think about this is to consider your house flooding. A flood would devalue your house due to the damage it caused. You therefore hedge against this risk by taking out house and contents insurance.

Hedging is also used to maximise overall performance and sustainability, especially when it comes to wealth-building liquidity. If you decide to activate all three tiers of your investment account like I did, you will benefit from maximum acceleration towards financial freedom. Once I learned to trade, I was able to replace my active income in just over three and a half years. With my wealth liquidity system complete, my focus was to water it as much as I could and make it sustainable.

There are a few things that you need to consider when managing a system like this:

- Steady, consistent growth
- Minimum drawdowns
- Sustainability

What I am about to share are considerations I recommend. However, they are optional and, of course, dependent on your personal preference.

How you manage your entire investment account overall will determine its rate of growth. At the time I was able to replace my active income, I was generating per annum on average 10% from passive investments, 15% on stocks and 36% in my trading. The cumulative growth of my entire investment account worked out at approximately 20% per year.

Dynamically hedging low-skill, low-time investments with high-skill, highly speculative investments not only allows me to benefit from maximum diversity and accelerated growth, but also provides me with flexibility to adapt my system to suit my changing motives and projects that come up. Here are some strategies to maximise growth by managing the entire liquidity system in unison.

Investing to speculation ratio

If you decide to allocate some of your investment account to the Tier 1 section, then the ratio will be dependent on how much you feel comfortable allocating. Depending on your time commitments and skills, you may decide to allocate a small amount such as 5% or 10%. As you get better at trading and find yourself with more free time, you may decide to increase that allocation.

There is no universal right or wrong here, as differing financial values and goals require differing ratios. As a general rule of thumb:

- More aggressive individuals will favour a higher percentage in trading (Tier 1).
- More conservative individuals will favour a higher percentage in investing (Tier 2).

While I cannot tell you exactly what T2:T1 ratio to use because it depends on your ability, where you are in your wealth journey and your risk tolerance, I recommend that you avoid becoming a 100% pure speculator. This is putting your eggs in one basket and building an upside-down pyramid. Instead, build the Tiers of Freedom®.

I suggest a maximum of 50% to be allocated to speculative trading. It's always best to start with a small percentage, between 5–10%, to keep below the maximum emotional fluctuation level that could jeopardise your wealth building. Once you have proved to yourself that you can generate consistent returns, you can then consider opening the tap a little to allow more liquidity into your Tier 1 account.

There is no maximum recommended limit on your Tier 2 passive investment percentage. In fact, you are likely to approach a 100% passive investment allocation under three circumstances:

- You temporarily lack the time for speculative trading among other duties and projects.
- You quit speculative trading permanently.
- You die.

A 100% passive investment allocation, under sound portfolio management, is a fine way to grow wealth. If another project arises, commands your attention and you value it more, give yourself permission to pursue it with all the energy it requires while temporarily using a higher-than-average passive investment allocation.

Let the results speak for themselves. Over time, the ultimate determinant of the T2:T1 ratio is your speculative performance. If your trading continues to massively outperform your passive investment portfolio, you will naturally gradually move towards a higher T2:T1 ratio. If your T1 account continues to stagnate or experience drawdown, you will naturally gradually move towards a lower T2:T1 ratio.

Update your T2:T1 ratio in gradual increments every six to twelve months to reflect your performance and ever-changing financial goals.

Don't get too top heavy

The aim is always to have the majority of your investment capital in Tier 3 and Tier 2, but as your speculation performance increases, Tier 1 will naturally outperform the lower returns of Tier 2 and Tier 3. This causes the entire pyramid to become top heavy.

To maintain a sustainable and long-lasting liquidity system, you'd be wise to regularly rebalance the capital across the three tiers proportionally. Once every twelve to twenty-four months, take stock of the capital across the entire investment account structure and consider withdrawing some of the Tier 1 and maybe Tier 2 funds and rebalancing distribution evenly.

Here's a hypothetical example. At the start of the year, you have these allocations:

Tier 3 – Cash = £50,000   50% allocation

Tier 2 – Index funds = £30,000   30% allocation

Tier 2 – Stocks = £20,000   20% allocation

Tier 1 – Forex = £10,000   10% allocation

By the end of the year, you have some good returns in your stocks and forex account. Your returns look like this:

Tier 3 – Cash = £50,500   1% ROI

Tier 2 – Index funds = £33,000   10% ROI

Tier 2 – Stocks = £23,000   15% ROI

Tier 1 – Forex = £14,000   40% ROI

By the end of year two, your returns look like this:

Tier 3 – Cash = £51,005   1% ROI

Tier 2 – Index funds = £36,300   10% ROI

Tier 2 – Stocks = £26,450   15% ROI

Tier 1 – Forex = £19,600   40% ROI

You can see that the Tier 1 account is now becoming top heavy as it represents almost 50% of your Tier 3 allocation. Another year of returns like these could mean that you have the majority of your portfolio allocation in speculation, which is not a good idea.

This is just a hypothetical example, but there could be times where you have a big win in your trading account or even a series of big wins. You could also experience a quick growth in one of your stocks.

In April 2020, I had my biggest trading day to date, generating over £133,000 in just under eighteen hours. Later that year, one of my crypto trades hit profit targets, resulting in a win of just over £227,000 in one trade. In these two sessions alone, I made more than my average annual returns in my speculation account and, as a result, my Tier 1 account became top heavy.

In January 2021, I carried out a rebalancing project on my entire portfolio to reallocate and distribute my capital to ensure it was diversified correctly. If you want to build sustainable long-term wealth and a real legacy, it is always wise to keep your pyramid bottom-heavy.

EXERCISE: Tier 2 rebalancing

Your T2:T1 ratio is a method of rebalancing your investment capital across the three tiers of the pyramid. Tier 2 rebalancing refers to the horizontal distribution of investment capital. This is essentially the distribution of your capital across asset classes.

It's a good idea to carry out this exercise every six to twelve months or, at most, when you carry out your tiered rebalancing. Why is this needed?

Sometimes, your stocks will outperform your bonds. Sometimes, your bonds will outperform your stocks. It is wise, therefore, to ensure your Tier 1 portfolio is balanced to reflect the asset allocation that you initially intended. I have developed a tool called the Wealth Atlas as part of my suite inside my Tiers of Freedom® programme that allows you to figure out very quickly and accurately how much should be held in each asset class. If you do not have access to that tool, you can use the method below.

Take a look at your investments and the performance of the returns on each asset. Identify the percentage you initially allocated to each asset class.

Use these figures to determine how much you need to top up your underperforming funds. In some cases, you may need to sell off some holdings in high-performing asset classes. Do this sparingly and only if the underperforming asset class is extremely out of balance to the upside.

When selling any assets within your Tier 2 investment account, familiarise yourself with any tax regulations that may apply. For example, if you're taxed at a lower rate for selling any holdings over twelve months old, it may pay to stretch out your portfolio balancing process to every 367 days.

Capital partitioning

Capital partitioning is an advanced management routine used by traders to hedge against risk in the Tier 1 section of their investment account.

When you build your T1 account to a significant level (whatever that might be for you), it can feel uncomfortable having all of your capital for that tier stored in one place. This can play on your mind and in turn jeopardise your performance.

Capital partitioning is a method of segregating the balance of your trading account so that you protect what isn't being used and don't have all of your available funds in one broker account. The most popular arrangement is a simple 50/50 split.

Here is how it works. If your Tier 1 trading account size is £100,000, you would move £50,000 into a high-interest-yielding investment account. You would then double your trade risk size in your reward to risk ratio for each trading position, pretending the account size was still £100,000.

This has two main benefits:

- Your capital is more secure since it is held in two separate accounts instead of one. In the extremely unlikely event that your broker 'loses' your money or your account is frozen, only half of your capital is at risk.

- You will actually earn a 'guaranteed' return from the half that sits in the high-interest-earning account. This can increase your overall return.

Since you will be trading double the risk on the £50,000 that remains in your trading account, this has the same effect as trading the normal risk on your initial

£100,000 account. Therefore, you will receive the benefits and security of diversifying your parked capital with no disadvantage to your trading activity at all.

Accelerating financial freedom

To put into context how powerful utilising both investing and trading strategies is for sustainable accelerated returns, I want to give you some numbers based on learning one trading strategy and implementing it in your overall wealth liquidity system. Take my daily time frame trend trading system as an example.

My daily swing trading system requires little time because I only need to check the charts once per day. The system has a strike rate of approximately 65%, meaning that I am right 6.5 times out of 10 on average.

I trade this strategy across twenty-seven different combinations of the major markets. Each week, due to the quality filters in the strategy, I get on average three or four opportunities – let's say twelve opportunities per month. With a 65% strike rate, that means out of twelve trades, I am likely to average eight wins and four losses per month over time.

If you were to trade this system limiting your risk to a maximum of 1% on any one trade with a reward to risk ratio of 1:1 (meaning you gain 1% on every winner), you would return a 4% gain in your account each month.

$$8 \text{ wins} - 4 \text{ losses} = 4 \text{ wins } (4\%)$$

You might say that 4% doesn't sound like much, but it actually compounds out to just over 60% per year. Check for yourself using the compound calculator here: http://bit.ly/afcompound

If I balance my portfolio allocations perfectly and I am returning 60% on my T1 account and 10% on my T2 account, this means that my entire liquidity system is growing at a steady average of around 40% per year. Not bad.

Let's say you only yield half of my results and generate an overall return of 20% per year. If you have built your wealth liquidity system properly and are implementing the rest of the strategies in this book, you will have complete income replacement within five years. That's without increasing returns (which is unlikely). Sound good? Of course it does.

If you had just £20,000 starting capital and took no deposits, in eight years of returning 60% per year, your account balance would compound out to approximately £1,000,000. If you then continue trading a £1m account with the same performance, you will be churning out £600,000 per year, which is roughly £40,000 per month just from your T1 account.

I like tangible numbers.

If you are able to generate those sorts of returns, you will have no trouble funding your account because you will be throwing as much as you possibly can at it. So will your family, so will investors.

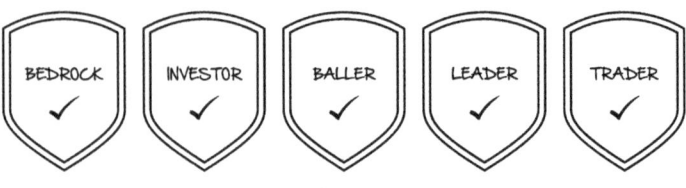

Earning your Trader Badge can allow you to see serious acceleration in your wealth. This is what enabled me to whittle my journey to financial freedom down to just three and a half years.

TOP TIP

Since you cannot actively trade after you die, be sure to leave instructions with your estate planner to move all remaining trading capital into your passive investment portfolio in the event of your death. Provide the basic allocation and balancing instructions so it can continue to build wealth centuries after you depart.

Your passive investment portfolio is a self-growing and willable asset that can be used to change the world well after you've finished your time here. This is why it is referred to as the 'long game'.

PART 5
BECOMING ALWAYS FREE

Your freedom has been inside of you since you were born.

When I became financially free, I realised all I wanted to do were things I would have done as a child. Fun stuff.

When I visited Disney World in 2012, as my family and I walked up to show our entry tickets to the old guy who worked on the gate, he said, 'Go be a kid again.' I remember thinking how meaningful that sentence was. There were literally thousands of excited people running through the gates, eager to go and be childlike. Happiness was everywhere.

What's sad is that most people reach their thirties and realise they 'should' have done what they always wanted to do as a child. They then become depressed over trying to figure out how they can get back to doing what they love every day.

Acknowledge that you are where you are today due to choices and decisions and actions you took because you thought there would be a payoff instead of pain. Then start becoming who you truly want to be by taking choices, decisions and actions that align with who you really are.

Life is too short to spend it being someone else. You are you and every ounce of freedom you desire is already inside of your mental, physical and spiritual capacity.

17
Scaling Your Lifestyle

One thing people never seem to consider is how to hedge their lifestyle and scale it in a way that is inspiring to them. They rarely have a strategy for scaling their lifestyle that avoids risking or sacrificing their liquidity and freedom.

How you scale your lifestyle can make or break your chance of achieving financial freedom. It is extremely important to have a way of managing your lifestyle alongside your wealth liquidity system so you can still have everything you want in life.

We are worthy of receiving all of the wealth and experiencing all the things we want to experience as a result of the love, creativity and value we share with the world. That means we do not need to scrimp or be tight with our money. It means we can have what we want at the right time.

The FREEDOM lifestyle scale formula

If you follow my FREEDOM lifestyle scale formula, you will have the best chance of getting what you want in life without sacrificing liquidity while still building sustainable wealth.

FREEDOM stands for:

- F – Fair exchange
- R – Rate of growth
- E – Expectations
- E – Expenses to assets
- D – Debt to income
- O – Other people's money
- M – Minimum splurge

Let's look at each element in a bit more detail.

Fair exchange

Fair exchange rules the game. Taking more than you give is an expectation against universal laws. If you are to build wealth, you must first accept you are going to have to give an equal proportion of output to the world in some form. Whether that's in a business, a job, a charity or community, you will get what you give. Those who give more, get more.

Fall in love with earning through service of some kind.

Rate of growth

When it comes to lifestyle, focus on steady, consistent and sustainable growth. I know many people who have a good year in business, and then go and spend a large lump of cash on a nice brand-new car, only to find that the next year isn't so good and they have to sell the car. They have continuous ups and downs, experience extreme highs and extreme lows.

This way of life is volatile and stressful. It's better to plan for goals and then grow your lifestyle according to those goals.

Expectations

Having real numbers based on the calculations I have given you will help you visualise what your future looks like financially rather than it being a fluffy dream with no direction. If you have tangible information plotted out on a graph, you can plan exactly when you will be able to afford certain things and how you are going to get them. This will significantly enhance your chances of achieving them and stop you from having the urge to make momentary splurges.

Expenses to assets

There is a ratio between your savings or LAs and your LEs, which is the balance between your freedom and your luxuries. Knowing this number and keeping the ratio balanced will allow you to maintain the feeling of prosperity while scaling your expenses to get the things you want, as I explained with the Freedom Formula in Chapter 9.

As a rule of thumb, never increase your LEs unless you can increase your regular savings and liquidity deposits by the same amount. This allows you to take on expenses without sacrificing your feeling of freedom.

Debt to income

We have already covered the DTI ratio in Chapter 9, but I can't stress enough the power of using this calculation to control the rate at which you take on non-cash-flow producing debts. Don't buy stuff you don't need on a whim and sacrifice your own mental health. Keep your DTI below 20%, and ideally 10%.

Other people's money

You may have heard people promote the use of other people's money and you may have heard others say things like, 'Debts are bad'. You already know the rules around cash-flow producing debts over non-cash-flow producing debts, so my rule of thumb here for borrowing other people's money is never to sacrifice your own liquidity if an alternative option exists.

It's common in my generation for people to save and save, and then spend all of that liquidity on a car or other expensive item. This is like relying on a tap to produce water, and then freezing the tap so it just drips. When people do this, they have to keep going to work to pay for the car that sits on the drive most of the week.

If you are investing passively in the markets each month and returning 7% per annum, it doesn't make sense to miss out on that 7% income to avoid paying the interest on finance, which is usually less than 7%. Otherwise, you would be losing income for the sake of ownership. My personal preference is to enjoy my lifestyle *and* drive the car, while retaining the liquidity to live freely.

The pride of ownership traps people too often. Renting a house rather than buying might be the better option for you. Getting a car loan might be the better option. If you don't do the maths, you won't know.

Minimum splurge

This is the final rule, which states that you can ignore the option of using other people's money if the purchase cost is less than 1% of your entire liquidity.

There will be occasions where it doesn't make sense to spend time and effort to arrange a loan or finances on a purchase. When your time is more valuable than the process, it doesn't make it financially viable.

My rule for this is 1%. If the purchase costs 1% or less of your entire liquidity, it makes sense just to make it with cash.

If you scale your lifestyle using these principles, you will accumulate all the luxuries and experiences you need in life without sacrificing your liquidity or freedom.

TOP TIP

Imagine you sat on a nail sticking up from the floor. It would feel extremely painful even if the nail was fairly blunt. This is because the surface area of the nail is so small compared to the surface area of your body.

On the other hand, if you lay on a bed of ultra-sharp nails, it wouldn't hurt because the load would spread over a larger area. In this respect, it's wise to think of your investments like a bed of nails.

18
The Time Is Now

You have potentially learned and digested a lot of information throughout this book that may seem esoteric and taking action on some of it may feel a little uncomfortable. Remember, if you want the life you dream of, you have to push the boundaries of your comfort zone.

This can naturally bring out a few fears. I say 'bring out' because the fears were already there before you picked up this book.

We often hear people say, 'I fear the unknown', but actually that's rubbish. A fear is simply an imagining of the future based on a negative perception of something that has happened in our past. In other words, our fear is based on an experience.

You may have grown up with parents arguing about money. You may have been mugged. You may have been scammed. You may have watched a scary film. Any of these things will cause your mind to project thoughts into the future that can potentially inject fear into you. The way to move forward is to pinpoint and get clear about any fears you might have and why you might have them. You can then dissolve fear by finding the benefits to the experience it's based on, how it served you instead of how it could hinder you.

What often hinders your self-improvement journey is fear. If you attach fear to the process, it will feel like hard work.

Let's imagine you draw two parallel lines on the floor in your hallway about one foot apart. Do you think you could stay within those lines while walking the entire length of your hallway? Of course you could.

Let's now say that instead of your hallway, you are on a one-foot-wide ledge 500 feet in the air and you have to walk across it. How would the task feel now? Harder? Of course it would, but is it really harder? No. It's the same exercise.

We all have a comfort zone. We like to live in that comfort zone. We feel comfortable and safe there. Once outside of the comfort zone, we think we will be exposed to more judgement.

I carried out a survey with my network and asked them what their current biggest fear was. Believe it or not, the fourth most common fear was of success and the limelight. This proved that people actually fear getting results.

The more money you make, the more success you have in business, the more people you serve, the more people will judge you. It's a fact.

Dissolving your excuses

Financial freedom takes courage. If you're not ready to deal with that and you have a strong fear about what other people are going to say, then you will keep playing a small game. It will be frustrating because you're trapped in your comfort zone. Every now and then, you'll push against the border of it and it will feel hard. It will feel painful and you'll think it's 'hard work'.

In this section, I'm going to share some of the most common reasons people give me for not embarking on their journey to financial freedom (and why they are not actually reasons to delay).

You will never have enough money

People tell me they will start their wealth creation journey when they have more money. This is a bit of a chicken and egg situation.

Here is the thing. We spend our money on what we value most. If you haven't valued wealth building to this point, you are not going to start spending money on it when you get more money. The entire time your emotions are choosing what to spend your money on, you will end up with more month at the end of your money than money at the end of your month.

It's a bit like people who don't value exercise and losing weight. They always aim to start Monday, but Monday is just a made-up day. Today is as good as any other day. If you need to set a date to start, you are only making yourself feel better about delaying the process by setting an excuse.

Get accountable, remove emotion and make a start. Today!

You will never have enough time

The same way you spend the majority of your money on what you value most, you also spend the majority of your time doing what you value most. You have probably just spent hours reading this book, so I know you are already dedicating time to wealth building, but when you put the book down, you risk never putting everything you have learned into action.

If you don't plan and fill your day with tasks that will move you forward in your wealth journey, it will get filled with everyone else's agenda and you will never find the time. Any time something comes up that feels even remotely more interesting than working on your financial freedom, you will take that option. The truth is, you will never find the time. You must make time. It's now or never.

When I learned to trade, I was running a business with seventeen full-time staff. I also had two kids and a wife I wanted to spend quality time with. To get some balance in my family life, I would get home from the office each day around 5pm, eat dinner and spend some time with my family until they went to bed. I would then start on my trading, which would take me from 11pm until 2am. I would do the same thing each and every day, as well as spending most Saturdays in the local coffee shop with my laptop.

Remove decisions from your agenda and put yourself first. No one else will ever tell you to ignore them and work on you. You have to do it now.

I recommend you do the time study exercise in Chapter 10 if you skipped it earlier. This will give you a heat map of exactly how much time you're spending on certain tasks in the week.

Waiting for debt to clear first

Many times, I have heard people say that they will start their wealth journey when they clear their debt. My advice, as I said earlier, is to do both simultaneously.

If you are in debt, you feel uninspired to save money. The thing is, as you pay the debt off, you will feel better and want to treat yourself. Believe it or not, you are at risk of getting back into debt just by paying your debt off.

Here is the thing: the habit of saving is far more important than the amount you are saving, especially in the early stages. Watching your money grow is much more inspiring than paying off debts. If you can do both at the same time and have an account that is forever growing, it will motivate you to keep it going, and once your non-cash-flow producing debt is paid off, you are far more likely not to take on any more.

Treat your savings like a debt payment. Pay yourself instead.

You will never be motivated

Motivation is a myth. People only feel motivated when they are doing something they are called from within to do. Something they are really inspired to do. When people say they are not motivated, what they really mean is they are in one of two categories.

1. What they are going after isn't that important to them. Believe it or not, in my experience about 80% of the people who are demotivated are not actually invested in what they are doing. They are likely looking up to other people, trying to get a result in an area that isn't inspiring to them.

2. Overwhelm. This is caused by not chunking down goals or processes into bite-sized pieces that are easy to tick off.

Usually what happens when we don't break down our goals is that we get overwhelmed by a tiny little task that we know needs doing, but we subconsciously don't want to do it. Because we haven't taken the time to identify it and delegate it, we procrastinate on the entire goal.

People you see who seem motivated are not motivated. They are simply doing what they love. When you see someone who looks like they have something special about them, that is not motivation. It's inspiration from within.

You now have a comprehensive plan to work on for your financial freedom. The way to achieve it is to spend time around others who are on the same journey. They will inspire you. Get around people who will hold you accountable to your goals. Create forfeits and contingencies to ensure you continuously move forward from this day onwards. Then you'll have access to all your untapped power and potential.

Hard work is a myth

You may feel like you have some work to do. Do not consider it hard. Financial freedom is actually a straightforward process and I hope this book has inspired you to take action on it.

The definition of hard work is literally a formula:

$$\text{Work} = \text{Force} \times \text{distance}$$

A teenage programmer sitting at his or her desk in a dark bedroom for an hour per day can earn more money and have more freedom than a roofer who has to work in the blazing summer sun. Roofing is demanding work on the body and coding requires little physical effort.

The amount of work that you put into something is literally the amount of force that you apply multiplied by the distance that you apply it. That's work. The 'hard workers' are the ones putting in the most force over the biggest distances.

If people are repeatedly putting in great amounts of work and they haven't come up with systems or tools or delegations not to have to do so, then they won't make more money because they haven't invested in their knowledge. It's got nothing to do with hard work; it's about lack of smart work.

Take action

As long as you are fit and healthy, the chances are you have many years left of your life. How much have you learned in your life so far? How much have you achieved?

Did you know that statistically, most people who become wildly successful do so after their forties?[51] This is because they have learned the fundamentals, made some mistakes which they now know to avoid, found a path that is right for them, and they then hit it out of the park. You have time to become financially free because it doesn't take that long if you apply what you have learned here...

Having said that, I don't want you to get too relaxed because you need to build the right habits. Reading this book isn't enough. Actions speak louder than words. Realising your goals all boils down to action and the steps you take.

If anyone says to you that knowledge is power, they're lying. Knowledge is only power if you apply what you learn and stop waiting for the perfect moment. There has never been a successful person who waited for the time to be right, the market to be right, their home life

---

51 P Azoulay, BF Jones, J Daniel Kim and J Miranda, 'Research: The average age of a successful startup founder is 45', *Harvard Business Review* (11 July 2018), https://hbr.org/2018/07/research-the-average-age-of-a-successful-startup-founder-is-45, accessed 15 April 2025

to be settled, their debts to be cleared, their family to be supportive, their job to be perfect and their bank account to be in the black. It has never happened.

When it comes to wealth building, people often overestimate what can be achieved in twelve months, but they also underestimate what can be achieved in twenty-four months. I hope this book has opened your eyes to what you can achieve and made you excited about your future.

Your life right now is a result of the decisions you've made and the actions you have taken in the past. The decisions you make and the actions you take today will dictate where you are five years from now.

The question is, where are you going to be? What is your time worth?

EXERCISE: Where do you need to be?

Write down your current annual income. Write down your ideal annual income. Then write down the difference between the two.

The answer is the error figure between where you are now and where you want to be in terms of income.

If you could definitely become Phase 2 – financially free in the next six to twelve months – how much of that error figure would you be willing to spend on that? What would that be worth to you?

The figure you get from this exercise is not for me to know. It's just a threshold for you to be aware of and think about before you start spending countless hours searching YouTube for the answers. You only have finite time on this planet and as the hours pass, your time becomes more and more valuable.

My advice is not to waste a minute of it.

In Part 1, I asked you to take a test. I invite you to go back to www.alwaysfree.com/fqtest and compare the results. Is your financial reality shifting?

TOP TIP

Write down the ten things that you're most afraid of being judged for by other people, and then make a start on doing them now.

Conclusion:
The Key Is Happiness

Over the years, I have found myself in the company of people in extreme poverty who have been raised in broken homes. They have turned to drugs, theft and a life of ruin where the rut they have got themselves into seems to shape their destiny.

I grew up thinking that poverty was only found in third-world countries or areas of economic ruin, but poverty is relative. Poverty is a situation whereby your ability to financially maintain the comforts you have become acclimatised to in life is out of your control and awareness.

I have worked with celebrities who cannot afford their new acclimatised comforts anymore. I have also met wildly successful people who have built multi-million pound businesses, and yet have turned to drugs and become extremely unhappy. I personally know of a millionaire who took his own life when everyone else thought he was the luckiest person on Earth. As sad as this was, I couldn't help but become fascinated with the patterns and relationships between money and happiness.

You can have no money and be unhappy. You can have lots of money and be unhappy. You can have no money and be happy. You can have lots of money and be happy.

The key is happiness.

I know what happiness is. It's being able to wake up every day choosing how I spend every minute of my time. It's being spontaneous and enjoying a breakfast beside a lake with my family on a Tuesday morning. It's being in full control of my life and not worrying about money. It's being able to have the experiences that are most important to me and creating memories with my family for the short amount of time we have together on this beautiful planet.

That is happiness.

The strategies in this book have allowed me to live and breathe happiness. If my life stays the same way it is now for the rest of my days, I will die an extremely happy man.

No resentment. No regrets. Just happiness.

The three freedoms

Your journey to happiness comes from mastering the strategies in this book and working on three freedoms.

The common view is that freedom is solely attributable to finances or money. You now know this is not entirely true. How much money you have and your level of financial freedom are completely different studies.

The fact is, how we spend our money is dictated by how we let others spend it for us. The ideas we have and the influences on how we manage what we earn usually come from advice from others, marketing campaigns, peer pressure etc.

Your route to happiness now lies in your ability to master these three freedoms:

1. Mental freedom. This is being able to digest advice from others, synthesise paradoxes and align the actions you take with your ideal life.

We all know people who just do not give a crap. They are inspiring. They don't care what others think of them. Anyone who doesn't allow other people's ideas to influence them away from their own true mission and values is already a very free human being.

2. Mobility freedom. If you are the type of person who is mentally free and you do what you choose to do every day, rather than basing it on what others want you to do, then the next important element of freedom is mobility. If you can do what you want wherever you want, you are one heck of a free individual.

3. Financial freedom. If you are doing what you want wherever you want, the chances are you won't ever want to stop, but supreme freedom comes from having the choice to stop should you wish or need to. That is where the financial element comes in. Financial freedom is what underpins your mental freedom and mobility freedom and gives you the choice to stop at any point. Albeit a small part of your overall feeling of freedom, it's still an important one.

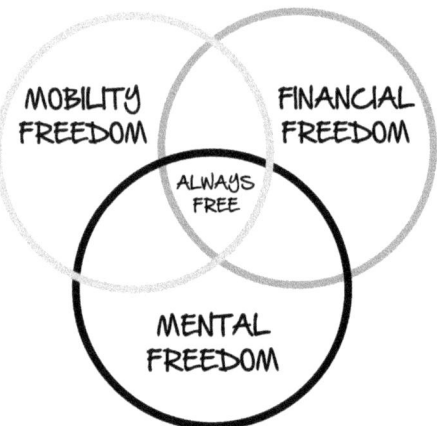

In summary, financial freedom is probably the least relevant contributor to your overall feeling of freedom. Interesting, eh?

CONCLUSION: THE KEY IS HAPPINESS

The thing is, most people figure out later in life that they haven't been mentally free for years. This has led them into a position whereby they are trying to figure out how to become financially free, but it's a chicken and egg situation. They are disconnected from their purpose and have little drive to actually achieve it.

There are many valuable concepts I hope you have learned from reading this book that will have an enormous impact on your finances and lifestyle. However, the most powerful advantage comes in the form of the hidden benefits. When you are able to free up your time, you naturally become a better human being. You become focused, you get clarity and what's more, you become extraordinarily self-aware of your untapped potential that opens up limitless opportunities.

TOP TIP

With most jobs or businesses, we want to provide value, feel fulfilled and be rewarded. Having too much or too little of one or more of these three things makes us feel either unethical, unrewarded or unfulfilled, so there needs to be a balance. This is why it can feel like there is something missing from your life when you become financially independent, because you no longer have to provide value.

The good thing is, with financial freedom, you can choose how you would like to provide value by focusing on something you are passionate about. When you are able to get the desire out of your head and provide value to someone else, you can live the most abundant life you could ever imagine.

Please keep me up to date on your journey progress from today onwards by visiting www.alwaysfree.com.

Here is to you becoming *Always Free*.

The Author

Jason Graystone is an entrepreneur, investor, author and host of the top-ranked *Always Free Podcast*. With hundreds of thousands of YouTube subscribers, Jason has become one of the most influential voices in the world of personal finance, trading and wealth creation.

Starting his first business at just twenty-two, Jason achieved financial freedom by thirty through a powerful combination of active income, smart investing and scalable business systems. Since then, he has built multiple seven-figure businesses and helped thousands of others pursue true financial independence through his industry-leading education programmes.

Jason has spoken on some of the world's most respected stages—from TEDx and leading universities to global investment summits and major corporations, including the Metropolitan Police. He's shared stages with some of the most iconic and celebrated figures in business and personal development.

In 2018, Jason was featured in *Forbes* for his innovative work in trader development, alongside renowned trading psychologist Dr Brett Steenbarger. His thought leadership continues to shape the financial education space globally.

Beyond business, Jason is a committed philanthropist, having helped raise hundreds of thousands of pounds for charitable causes. He believes that **everyone deserves to live an inspired life**—free to focus on meaningful work, creativity and contribution.

'When we're financially free,' he says, 'we become better human beings. The key to freedom is finding the sweet spot between fulfilment, reward, and inspiration. That's what it means to be always free.'

Jason has created all the illustrations in this book.

To find out more about Jason's work or connect with him go to www.alwaysfree.com.

www.ingramcontent.com/pod-product-compliance
Lightning Source LLC
Chambersburg PA
CBHW040519220526
45473CB00013B/2919